The Truth About Cora Pearl

Why cannot we be buried as eggs in neat little cells with ten or twenty thousand pounds each, wrapped round us in Bank of England notes, and wake up, as the Sphex wasp does, to find that its papa and mama have not only left ample provision at its elbow but have been eaten by sparrows some weeks before it began to live consciously on its own account?

The Way of all Flesh
SAMUEL BUTLER (1835-1902)

The Truth About
CORA PEARL

by
POLLY BINDER

WEIDENFELD & NICOLSON
LONDON

Published in Great Britain by
George Weidenfeld & Nicolson Limited
91 Clapham High Street
London SW4 7TA

ISBN 0 297 78590 7

Filmset by Deltatype, Ellesmere Port
Printed in Great Britain by
Butler & Tanner Ltd
Frome and London

Contents

DEDICATION
To my daughter
Josephine

Acknowledgments

I have found *The Pearl of Plymouth* by W. H. Holden useful, – all Joanna Richardson's books on the Second Empire helpful, – Alistair Horne's *The Fall of Paris* and S. Krachauer's *Jacques Offenbach ou le secret du Second Empire* most illuminating.

For hard facts I have consulted reliable Henry Mayhew. For hard visual facts I have studied Daumier and Constantin Guys. It is, I feel, necessary to correct the fulsome flattery, denunciation and spite of the French gossip-writers, and the inaccuracies of *The Times* and the *D.N.B.*

To my encouraging family, forbearing husband, and indomitable secretary, Jean Collins, my grateful thanks.

POLLY BINDER

I

Gossip and Scandal

For more than a decade, at the height of the glittering Second Empire, Paris adored the English courtesan known as Cora Pearl.

Everything she said, did, wore and did not wear, was news. Her cosmetics, her eyelashes, her dinner parties, her masquerade balls, her dogs, her stables, her *bons mots*, her equestrian expertise, her po-faced English grooms, her pet pig, kept the Paris gossip-column writers hard at work, their rent paid and their families fed and clothed.

'Her dresses and jewellery,' reported the glossy Paris magazine *Les Femmes du Jour*, 'are worth a million francs' (an under-estimate).

'She is the last word in luxury,' cried Prince Gortschakoff – 'I assure you I would try to pilfer the sun if that would satisfy a whim of hers.'

A famous Paris restaurant invented a new drink in her honour – '*Larmes De Cora*'.

In the French gossip magazine *Les Plaisirs de Paris*, Alfred Delvau wrote (in 1867):

You are today, Madame, renowned, the pre-occupation, the scandal and the toast of Paris. Everywhere they talk only of you – the humble to envy you, the wealthy to scorn you, the average people to adore you . . .
I content myself by putting your name like a rose-coloured flag at the portal of this little frolicsome temple raised in honour of Parisian pleasures of which you appear to be the most exquisite, the fullest and the dearest personification.

Yet only five years after this eulogy the Paris Press turned violently against her, hounding her out of Paris.

After pretending, during her lifetime, that she did not exist, England vented its spite after her death. *The Times* published a short obituary – hostile, mealy-mouthed and inaccurate. The *D.N.B.* accorded her the accolade of one and a quarter columns – bland, inaccurate and chiefly concerned with calculating how much money she had earned.

Biographies of this lady, nearly all written by men, contrive to be snobbish, prurient and boring all at the same time. Indeed, it must be said that they tell us more about the writers than about their subject.

Her own autobiography, written in French in her last years, when she was already gravely ill, is sadly muddled and confused; fading reminiscences of a vanished era, outmoded slang, merry anecdotes no longer merry, about long-forgotten socialites and pranks with royals whose thrones had long vanished. Even as she was writing she realized this, and confesses candidly that she has no literary ambitions but needs the money the publisher has offered. Yet even in this tired effort of recall there are sudden flashes of brilliant clarity, when her life is illuminated as by lightning – what she believed in, what she lived for, what she died by.

Cora Pearl's extraordinary career can only be understood by studying the social conditions in London and in Paris in the second half of the nineteenth century. For many thousands of young girls in London whose families could not afford to maintain them, the prospects were grim. Domestic servants were very ill paid, endured very long hours of work with hardly any time off. The needle trades: sewing shirts or dresses for very low wages, with no security were worse. Milliners were also paid starvation wages for very long hours of work and it was accepted that the girls would eke out their wages by going on the streets. They were known as 'dolly mops' who, while their youth lasted, could hope for an occasional evening's fling and a free supper.

Marriage for poor girls was no rosy alternative – who would have them but equally ill-paid unskilled workmen? All they could then look forward to was the prospect of a large brood of underfed children to rear.

The cards fate dealt out to these penniless girls were the same.

How the girl played them depended on her intelligence, her luck, and above all on her character.

The number of prostitutes haunting mid-Victorian London was around 80,000. There was no police control except in the notorious dance-halls. As to the wealthy and the nobility, they did whatever they chose with impunity, for the dogged British axiom that 'a man's home is his castle' blocked every well-meaning attempt to regulate this traffic, from which even children were not immune.

To be set up in a smart villa in Hammersmith, or a pretty two-storey house in St John's Wood or, best of all, a *bijou* mansion in Mayfair, was the dream. Out of 80,000 competitors very very few ever made the dream a reality.

Unlike London, Paris endeavoured to regulate its prostitution. The official number of prostitutes in Paris at this period was 53,000. These 'girls' (who gave themselves such fancy names as 'Sidonia', 'Artemisia', 'Octavia', or, further down the ladder, 'Boulotte', 'Faux-cul', 'Belle-cuisse'), were issued with official licences and obliged to submit to regular medical inspection. But there were also much larger numbers of unregistered prostitutes in Paris.

Not surprisingly venereal diseases were rampant, both in London and Paris, and as medication was primitive, many died horribly of them. Amongst those who died in France were Baudelaire, de Maupassant, and the younger of the Goncourt brothers. Théophile Gautier caught syphilis whilst he was the Duc de Morny's secretary – and the understanding Duc gave him leave of absence to try to get himself cured which fortunately he managed to do.

In England, many good people, including a few clergy, tried to set up 'Societies for the Suppression of Vice' in order to protect some of the young girl victims. But these societies never lasted. Money soon ran out and their organisers were trounced in the press for their interference. Mission work abroad was highly commendable. At home it was not.

Gladstone tried to rescue some of these 'fallen doves' but what could he and Mrs Gladstone offer them instead? Prayers, penitence and maybe a dismal job in domestic service? It was hardly an attractive alternative to prostitution.

Actors, actresses and singers were not then socially acceptable either in London or in Paris, particularly singers. Queen Victoria and her music-loving Consort, it is true, liked to sing duets at home.

This wholesome example was faithfully followed by the English middle and lower-middle classes. But it had to be strictly amateur. Professional musicians were regarded with suspicion as was the theatre. Religious music (such as amateur church choirs) was as far as respectable families could go in England.

Thomas Bowdler had snipped the plays of Shakespeare into censored versions 'suitable for family reading'. But the theatre itself was definitely 'not respectable'. Even Lewis Carroll (the Reverend Charles Lutwidge Dodgson) who adored the theatre, had grave doubts about the propriety of theatre-going. He advised a friend, who had similar doubts, to think of himself actually dying in the theatre. Was it a suitable place from which to go and meet his maker? Surely it was not.

In Napoléon III's Court in Paris his mistresses were invited to banquets and fancy-dress balls, where the Court ladies were often free with their favours. But actresses and singers were never allowed into the Tuileries.

In its curious glittering way the Court of Louis-Napoléon, despite the marvellous toilettes and wonderful jewels and famous beauties, was just as dull and boring as Queen Victoria's respectable Court. The fun, the wit, the talent with which Paris abounded in that extraordinary epoch, were all bubbling outside the Court. And it was precisely the fun Paris offered outside the Court that the millionaires and royalty from every corner of the world flocked to Paris to enjoy.

And highest on the list of Paris fun-makers was Cora Pearl.

2
The Crouch Family

'Well then, I was born in 1842,' Cora Pearl declared in her memoirs, 'in Plymouth in Devonshire. My father was a composer of music, my mother a singer and so were my sisters. A family of performers. Sixteen children! Music and patriarchy. Biblical!' (Cora was probably including her mother's second family, and also a ten-year-old girl named Augusta Pearson, a relation of Mrs Crouch's who lived with them.)

'Cora Pearl' was the second daughter of Professor William Nicholls Crouch and his wife Lydia (Pearson) Crouch. She was christened Emma Elizabeth. Her elder sister, Ciantha, was born in London. After Emma Elizabeth, a third daughter, Hannah Lydia, was born in Plymouth. A fourth daughter, Charlotte, was also born in Plymouth, but at a different address. Less than two years later a fifth daughter, Louisa Elizabeth, was born in the same Plymouth house where Emma had been born. There was also a son, William, and an indispensable skivvy (probably a waif from the orphanage) named Emma Peckham.

The Crouches were forever moving house. To avoid creditors? In the hope of making a better living? 'Professor' Crouch (was he really a Professor?) counted distinguished musicians amongst his ancestors and had received an excellent musical education himself. His ambitions were as great as his livelihood was meagre.

Teaching singing to suburban daughters in the provinces must have irked him. Nor were his earnings sufficient to maintain his growing family. In between pregnancies and struggling to run her household on insufficient means, Mrs Crouch also gave singing lessons.

His eye always on the elusive pot of gold at the foot of the rainbow, Professor Crouch was forever fossicking through ladies' magazines, hunting for ballads which he could set to music, and dazzling his children with tales of his adventurous youth and early musical triumphs. At the age of nine, he boasted, he had played in the orchestra of the Royal Coburg Theatre – later he had played in the orchestra of the Drury Lane Theatre, and had sung in the choirs of St Paul's Cathedral and Westminster Abbey. And they must never forget that their grandfather, Frederick William Crouch, had taught music to the Duke of Clarence who became King William IV of England.

There was another side to Professor Crouch's romantic history, that of the intrepid adventurer. During a period of poverty he had bravely signed on a coastal trawler as common seaman. And there was yet another side: brilliant industrial inventor. He had become a metal broker and invented a wonderful new process of working zinc, in which, unfortunately, he had lost all his savings. And now he was about to become rich and famous by composing immortal songs and operas.

Little Emma listened, entranced. All this was better than a fairytale. She knew she was her father's favourite daughter and that he was indeed going to become rich and famous.

A Micawber family always expecting something to turn up. Poor Mrs Crouch had heard it all so often. As she packed up their flimsy belongings for yet another move, she knew her husband would never put down roots, that he was useless as a provider and that his dreams of wealth and fame grew ever more grandiose as his earnings dwindled. Mrs Crouch turned to God in despair. No-one else could help, and she longed above all to keep her family respectable.

And when Professor Crouch's great chance came, and the pot of gold for which he had searched so long was actually within his grasp, he muffed it.

He had picked out a sentimental little ballad by Mrs Louisa Matilda Jane Crawford from the *Metropolitan Magazine*. It was called 'Kathleen Mavourneen', and he set it to music. He played this composition to Mr and Mrs Rowe, printers of music in Plymouth. To his joy they liked it enough to agree to publish it, and, never one to read the small print, he blithely signed away all his rights and royalties for £5. The song soon became popular – eventually world-famous. Every hurdy-gurdy clanked it out in every street for years. It is still popular. The publishers made at least £15,000 – a great fortune then – and later sold their copyright for a handsome figure.

Professor Crouch had already realized that his second daughter, Emma, had 'star quality', and he began to pay court to her. He was essentially a ladies' man and here he had just the kind of girl he needed to believe in his genius, in his masculinity, in his charm and in his great future. Moreover, though still only a little girl, Emma brimmed over with the qualities he found irresistible in the female sex.

Emma was radiantly healthy, her hair was red and curly, her cheeks rosy, her nose freckled. She had a beautiful skin and perfect teeth. She was a bouncy, bossy little girl – a bit of a tomboy – full of pranks and afraid of nothing. Crouch, proud of his Emma Eliza, took her about with him everywhere he went. He could not fail to observe that men – all manner of men – were immediately attracted to her. No doubt poor Mrs Crouch took great pains to dress Emma Eliza as well as she possibly could, and Emma loved clothes.

Years later Mr Rowe's piano-tuner remembered her vividly: 'Fine musician, Nicholls Crouch, and his daughter, Emma, a vivacious and charming girl then.'

Emma knew her father needed her admiration and support and they were always there for him, no matter how awry his business, how unappreciative the thin audiences for his lectures on Irish songs. Emma, vigorously applauding, willing him success, was the audience he performed for.

At home she was the natural leader of her family. She sang everything her family sang and practised scales by running her fingers up and down the large family ironing board in imitation of her adored father working out his compositions at the piano.

An emotional fixation in childhood such as Emma experienced can be disastrous or it can be fulfilling, either way it effectively prevents any other deep attachment developing.

Crouch's mother had also been a singer. Widowed, she soon married again, a musician, of course, but on the steadier administrative side. Mr William Watts, secretary of the Philharmonic

Society, was a good trustworthy man and compiler of the works of Lord Byron in several volumes.

When Professor Crouch was declared bankrupt, his mother cannot have been surprised for she knew his failings very well. Sharing Mrs Watts' anxiety about her son's lack of success and chronic instability, Mr Watts used his influence to obtain a job for his stepson, this time on the stage. The play was *Macbeth*. The theatre was the Haymarket. The fine cast included Charles Kean and Ellen Tree. Crouch was given a walk-on part.

The family was now lodged in London in dingy rooms in Fitzroy Street and Crouch came home less and less often.

Professor Crouch failed. He got the sack and played Hecate no more. He had come to a crisis in his life – his debts were increasing, his family (including his beloved Emma) had become an unwanted burden. Professor Crouch simply disappeared. He abandoned everything and fled to America in 1849 – then, as now, the land of golden dreams to indigent Europeans.

Mrs Watts, sensible and practical, hurried round to Fitzroy Street, after sending the children out with the skivvy, and took firm control of the impossible situation. She advised Mrs Crouch to announce that her husband had died and find means of bringing up the children to earn their livings. Mrs Crouch must try to marry again.

We can imagine poor Mrs Crouch in tears – protesting that she could not afford food for the children let alone the cost of mourning for their supposedly dead father.

Mrs Watts was made of sterner stuff and it must surely be from her that Emma inherited that strength of character and purpose which was to carry her later to success as Cora Pearl. The chief snag Mrs Watts foresaw to Mrs Crouch's remarriage would be Emma, for Emma, she knew, adored her father and would not accept a stranger in his place.

Ciantha, thanks to Mr Watts, had already obtained an engagement at Covent Garden and could support herself. The younger children must be supported until they could be apprenticed to some trade or other. Emma, brilliant, wilful headstrong Emma, must be got out of the way for a few years – and she must learn a useful trade to equip herself to earn her living. (One daughter eventually took a domestic job in Scotland and married the butler. Two other daughters became governesses – one in Prussia, the other in America. The youngest daughter, Louisa Elizabeth, became a well-known ballad singer in the music-halls. The son probably went into the Navy.)

Although she attracted men, Emma was not the type men would want to marry when she grew up. She was never going to grow into the sweetly pretty, modest maiden with smooth glossy hair, large eyes and small mouth that Victorian young men married. Her eyes were too small and her mouth was too big. She was a tomboy who would grow into a hoyden. And, the final bar to any hopes of marriage, she was penniless with no hope of a dowry.

So Mrs Watts unfolded her plan – Emma must be sent to France for a few years, to a respectable convent school *pension*, where she would learn French and book-keeping. Thus equipped, she could, on her return to England, be apprenticed to a good millinery establishment where she would in time become the manageress. And Mrs Watts would pay the fees for the French convent school. She had already located a suitable one in Boulogne.

Mrs Crouch agreed to all Mrs Watts' plans. The children were now told of their father's 'death'.

The shock to Emma was profound. She ran away to her shared attic bedroom and locked the door to weep her heart out.

Emma had been troubled by her father's increasing absence from home for some time, 'looking for work' or 'learning his part' or hunting for publishers for his two operas, *Sir Roger de Coverley* and *The Fifth of November*.

'Unhappily my father was a spendthrift,' Cora recorded in her memoirs. 'He loved us very much, no doubt, but was so careless with money that it no sooner came into our house than it flew out again. By the time he died he had wasted two fortunes. I was only five. [Cora was vague about dates and was probably about seven at the time.] I deeply missed my father.'

He was gone. He was dead. He had left her no letter, no sign, no word – nothing. He had abandoned her completely. She had given her heart forever to a man who had not deserved it. Hereafter she would love no man. Her father had freed her for good from the burden of love. He had locked that door forever and thrown away the key.

3
Education

Emma was duly packed off to the convent school in Boulogne to acquire French and book-keeping – it was also hoped she would shed her tomboy behaviour but, chiefly, they wanted to get her out of the way. It was almost certainly a catholic school but Emma stubbornly remained a protestant all her life.

Used to the bustle and tussle of a large family, she enjoyed her new life. A natural leader and born entertainer, Emma more than held her own with the other pupils. Her red hair, love of practical jokes and school-girl japes made her popular, and when speaking French her English accent was regarded as so comic that she clung to it for the rest of her life. She quickly became fluent and could, when she wished, speak perfect French. Coming from a dynasty of musicians her ear was perfect.

Emma immediately took to book-keeping for she had a natural passion for order. Order – Disorder. All her life Emma was to juggle expertly with these two sides of her character. The clean hands and tidy pinafore she presented for inspection after some riotous prank in the school dormitory, was a dress-rehearsal for cleaning up after a riotous dinner-party later on in her career. Top marks for tidiness. Bottom marks for behaviour.

Emma gave herself a cold sponge-down every morning. She enjoyed it. She was a strong, active and athletic child. She despised the *frieuse* French girls who molly-coddled themselves. Emma persisted and kept up her cold sponge-downs when, in the course of her career, the enamel jug and meagre convent wash-basin changed to less austere toilet equipment and finally, at the height of her fame, to the glories of her bathrooms in her Paris mansions and her country château.

Emma was popular with her class-mates and her teachers liked her. She enjoyed her schooldays and was sorry to leave them behind when the time came to return to London. Years afterwards she remembered with affection the appearance and idiosyncrasies of the convent staff.

Now, with fluent French, good marks in book-keeping and, hopefully, a more ladylike demeanour, Emma was to be put on the road to becoming manageress of a millinery emporium by her grandmother Watts, and thus able to earn a respectable living for herself one day.

Meanwhile Mrs Crouch had done as Mrs Watts advised and married again. Introduced by her mother-in-law into a circle of respectable people, the old lady's plan had worked. Mrs Crouch's second marriage was, of course, bigamous, but who was to know that? Her new friends were told that the brilliant Professor Crouch had died in America. And Mrs Watts would whisper to likely candidates for the now vacant post, how painful it was for poor widowed Mrs Crouch to be reminded of her sad loss every time the hurdy-gurdy in the street outside played 'Kathleen Mavourneen'.

Emma could understand and sympathise with her mother's dilemma.

'My mother had remarried,' Cora wrote in her memoirs, 'she needed support for her children, for those already in existence and a father for those still to come. It was this practical moral reason which decided my mother to make a new marriage.' She added, 'I cordially detested the second husband.'

Now that Emma was back in England and had made the acquaintance of her new step-sisters and step-brothers, it was decided that she should go and live with Mrs Watts, whose snug little villa was mercifully a good distance from her mother's home.

There are no lies in Cora Pearl's memoirs. She forgets names and confuses dates, not by design but because she was in pain and near her end, and her memory was fading. There was only one part of her life of which she ever felt ashamed and which she deliberately excluded from her memoirs. Indeed, we only know of it from letters written after her death by someone who knew her and her family at this time and had been at school with Emma's younger sisters.

This part of Emma's life, which she regarded as too humiliating to include in her memoirs, was her apprenticeship to a fashionable millinery emporium in Regent Street.

Mrs Watts' careful plans for Emma's future hurt Emma where she was most vulnerable. For Professor Crouch had always assured his lively little favourite daughter that her red curls, her vivacity and her charm, were going to carry her to the top of fashionable London society; where Dukes, Earls and Viscounts were thick as autumn leaves,and where her marvellous gowns and dazzling jewels would be the talk of the town.

Emma was determined to become what her papa had prophesied, but an apprenticeship in a millinery emporium seemed to her a step in the wrong direction. However in fashionable Regent Street she would be sure to meet the great ladies and their titled husbands. That would be a start. Emma promised herself that she would study their clothes, their accents, their conversation, their behaviour – everything.

But the emporium in Regent Street to which Mrs Watts' servant escorted Emma every day (for London streets were no place for a young girl walking alone), gave Emma a rude jolt. The reality of being a milliner's apprentice was anything but glamorous. Emma had to begin like all the other girl apprentices, by unpicking black linings from endless black mourning bonnets – wearying the eyes and depressing the spirit. After months of this she graduated to helping assemble the ingredients of pretty little bonnets she would have liked to wear herself, and awesome caps the emporium made for haughty society dowagers.

The manageress was a huge dragon in black bombazine who bullied the young apprentices and fawned on the haughty old dowagers. The customers for the delicious bonnets Emma coveted were gay young cockney girls who painted their faces and sported extravagant dresses. Their paramours who accompanied them, paid the bills.

Emma drank it all in.

Emma was not the success with her fellow apprentices that she had been with her school-mates in Boulogne. There was no time for comic turns and pranks. The dread eye of the manageress was forever upon them and the girls feared her. No snob, Emma nevertheless felt superior to these uneducated half-starved young apprentices, who snatched at the chance of going on the loose after work and never thinking beyond the evening's pleasure and a proper supper.

When the bombazine dragon was absent from the workroom toadying to rich clients, whom Emma never served despite her fluent French (for she was not the pale obsequious type of 'pin'-girl chosen to accompany the dragon into the fitting room), the apprentices giggled and gossiped about their favourite rendezvous, the Argyll Rooms, a dance hall in Windmill Street. Dolly-mops were beneath Emma's social aspirations, and she kept herself to herself.

Bonne maman, as Emma liked to call her grandmother Watts, was surely making a mistake. Millinery was the wrong career for Emma. She must think of something else. In the meantime Emma lived quietly with her in her neat suburban villa, playing cards with her in the evenings and reading the old lady to sleep with the adventure stories *bonne maman* so much enjoyed and which Emma found so boring.

The old lady felt her age and was taking things quietly. She had rescued her daughter-in-law and her family from the shambles her son had left them in, and she felt entitled to rest. However, there was one thing she absolutely insisted on – Emma was never allowed out alone. London was much too dangerous. On weekdays, therefore, Emma was always accompanied to and from the emporium by Mrs Watts' servant.

On Sundays, Emma, escorted by this same servant, visited her mother, who piously sent Emma to morning service at St James' church, Covent Garden, where, as Lydia Pearson, she had married Professor Crouch long ago. The servant accompanied Emma, left her at church for the service and brought her back afterwards. If Emma's step-father was away from home Emma stayed all day, romping with her family of sisters, brothers, step-sisters and step-brothers. If he was home the servant took Emma straight back to Mrs Watts' villa.

St James' Church (frequented by famous actors) was in an area of Covent Garden which, at that period, was far from respectable. Undesirable characters haunted the streets even in daytime. There were drinking dens and unsavoury eating houses, which were also brothels and worse.

'The following event,' wrote Emma, long long afterwards in her memoirs, 'decided my destiny . . . The maid who had accompanied me to church was not waiting to accompany me when I came out of church at the end of the service. She was late returning from her walk.

'I thought what fun it would be to return to Mrs Watts by myself – like a grown-up . . . So I started on my way, trotting along, prayer book in hand *"le nez au vent"* . . . I was followed. The man must have been about forty years old. It was like a scene from Red Riding Hood. He accosted me.

' "Where are you going little girl?"

' "To my grandmother, Sir."

' "Does your grandmother live near here?"

' "Oh! no Sir!"

'Then he said, "I am sure you like cakes." '

Emma blushed, smiled and did not reply.

Not yet fourteen, she was wearing a short dress and her red hair in a schoolgirl plait. She followed the well-dressed stranger. What could be more respectable than his heavy black whiskers, solid gold watch chain with heavy gold fobs, and fatherly manner?

' "Come with me," he said, "I will give you some!"

'What a windfall! How kind some people can be! How my *bonne maman* will laugh when I recount this adventure! After this, surely she will let me go out unescorted – all by myself. There really is no danger. So I followed the kind gentleman.'

The kind gentleman took Emma to a large house nearby – a cake shop, by the look of the front window. At the street corner there was a beggar child in rags to whom Emma gave a penny.

Inside the house was a bar-room, full of tobacco smoke. The gentleman seated Emma at a table, sat down himself and lit his pipe. Emma recalled waiting impatiently for her promised cakes, choked by the smoky atmosphere and upset by the noise. She did not like the place at all, and, when the gentleman went in search of cakes, she thought this was a good opportunity to run away. What kept her from leaving, she recounts, was her pride. She was a young lady now and must not behave like a frightened little girl.

The gentleman returned with a glass of sickly sweet *grog au rhum*, which Emma drank. By the time the cakes arrived her head felt like lead and her heart was thudding. She collapsed unconscious in her chair, the cakes untasted.

Emma recovered consciousness next day to find herself in a big bed with the gentleman beside her. There was blood on the disordered sheets. She was in pain.

The gentleman gave her money, said he liked her and she could stay with him. He offered to treat her to a tour of London. She refused. He put on his clothes and sat twiddling his thumbs. Then he put on his hat, shrugged his shoulders, laughed and left, saying, as he closed the door behind him: 'I never force anyone.'

Emma recorded that all she felt at that moment was overwhelming disgust:

I have never forgiven men, neither this man who had drugged and violated me, nor all other men who were not responsible. Now when I read the infamies reported in the *Pall Mall Gazette* I am not surprised. They still behave today exactly as they used to behave.

The paedophile who had violated her was a diamond merchant from Bordeaux. His name was Mr Saunders.

4
A Door Closes – A Door Opens

We do not know what happened when Emma failed to return to Mrs Watts' villa that fateful Sunday. Possibly Mrs Watts thought Emma had gone to stay with her mother overnight and her mother believed that Emma had gone back to Mrs Watts. By the time it was realized Emma was missing, valuable time had been lost.

Bringing in the police was the last thing they would have resorted to. And Emma's distraught mother had so many other younger children to keep her closely occupied. As to Mrs Watts, perhaps she travelled to the millinery emporium to make enquiries. Certainly there would have been a frosty reception. Emma had not been an ideal apprentice. It was inexcusable to disappear without giving notice and to break her indentures, etc.

Did the family hope and pray Emma would one day return to them, gay and lively as ever? Certainly Emma's mother would have prayed earnestly every night for her safety. Corpses were frequently fished out of the Thames. Often they were girls – either murdered or who had drowned themselves. Emma's mother would not let herself think about such bitter endings. Emma was so bright and so resourceful. Some day she must return. Meanwhile, there was prayer – so she prayed.

Emma was now on her own. In the respectable convention of Victorian England and the taboos of her Boulogne convent school, she had been brought up in ignorance of the facts of sex of which, she confesses in her memoirs, she knew 'rien de rien'.

In the aftermath of this sordid encounter, she was forced to realize what had been done to her and that, for the rest of her life, she would never set foot again either in her mother's home or in *Bonne maman*'s snug villa.

She disclosed in her memoirs:

Was I distressed? No. Regretful perhaps. I determined to always be honest with myself. I should lie if I said I wept at the pain of breaking away from my family. I had liked my boarding school better than my family.

But, though inexperienced, I felt that independence was best of all . . .

Nobody was going to be responsible for Emma from now on, except herself. No more prayers from her mother. No more good advice from her grandmother. No more escorting maid-servants. No more venom from the bullying manageress. In a surge of self-confidence Emma began to plan her future. Her resources? A prayer book and the money the diamond merchant had given her. Now she counted it. Five pounds. A fortune!

Not far from the *pâtisserie* where her violater had taken her, there was a modest boarding-house letting cheap rooms to respectable male shop assistants and working girls.

Emma took herself there and rented a furnished room. The landlord, a huge foreign-looking man, was respectful, Emma remembered, when she paid him the required rent in advance; he had observed that her speech and manner were superior to those of his other lodgers.

Emma next bought herself some necessary 'adult' clothes from a second-hand shop, choosing with prudence and a sharp practical sense which astonished her, half a century later, when she recalled her first steps to independence.

And now Emma took a most important decision. She changed her name. Nothing indicates so clearly her teenage dreams at this time than the name she invented for herself. 'Cora Pearl'. It breathes of autograph album school-girl fantasies. It is the kind of name her romantic father surely would have liked.

Emma, or Cora as we must now call her, installed herself in her rented room with joy and pride. It contained a bed, a table and a small cupboard.

Carefully dressed in her new second-hand clothes, Cora now made her way to the Argyll Rooms in Windmill Street, whose proprietor was Robert Richard Bignell. These dancing/dining rooms, furnished like a gin palace with opulent velvet benches, showy plate glass, much gilding and fancy gasoliers, were a popular, indeed notorious, rendezvous for harlots and their well-to-do clients. The entrance fee was one shilling, just within the reach of aspiring dolly-mops. The food and drink were expensive.

Bignell had worked his way up from boot-making to his present highly profitable position as owner of the Argyll Rooms, which he ran very well. He had introduced a popular new drink, the 'sherry cobbler', which gave strangers the opportunity to get together, for it was drunk from one glass with two straws.

Bignell worked hard at his profession. His rooms were well conducted. He himself was well dressed, good looking and pleasant mannered, with just the right touch of authority. He spoke French, essential in his career, which dealt in the exploitation of *filles de joie*.

His domestic life was as tragic as his professional life was successful. His wife (illiterate and unstable) had died in a stupid carriage accident. One of his two daughters was a lunatic. His splendid house in Kew afforded him little comfort, and he was lonely.

The moment Cora entered the Argyll Rooms that first evening, Bignell spotted her. He was, like so many other men throughout her life, instantly attracted by her red curls, her freckles, her lively expression and vigorous young body. Bignell kept Cora for himself, shielding her from the lecherous aristocrats who patronised the Argyll Rooms.

Cora remembered him afterwards with affection, and put his age down as twenty-five when they met, so he must have appeared young to her. In fact he was forty-five. He was gentle and helped her recover from her rape. He was, she wrote, 'madly in love' with her. The father–daughter relationship which was to recur again and again in Cora's life – with its hint of incest – bound them together.

But Cora was permanently immune from falling in love or loving any other man than her father. This was to be the determining factor in her success story.

Remarkable women (and history offers not a few who have made outstanding careers for themselves), often build their careers on the ruins of a shattering, emotional sexual experience. They then pour all their energy and released emotion into their careers. They will not, and do not seek to, love again. This was Cora's lot and she was lucky that her experience happened so early in her life, leaving her free and independent to pursue her extraordinary career – in a highly professional style.

Bignell felt for Cora, she wrote, *'une vive tendresse'*. They spoke French together. With their different English accents, that must have been delightful.

'He did not inspire me with passion,' Cora recorded, 'but by his delicacy and kindness, consoled me for the odious behaviour of the old satyr' (the diamond merchant).

An idyllic period followed, all that autumn, with quiet rustic dinners at village inns. Cora loved their autumn walks, gathering up fallen chestnuts and stringing them into long necklaces. She was nearly fifteen by now.

One day Mr Bignell proposed that Cora accompany him on a business trip to Paris. Cora was delighted at the prospect of such a treat. All she knew of France was the convent school in Boulogne.

Bignell procured a new passport made out in the name of 'William Bignell travelling with his wife'. Fancy him thinking of that, the sly boots! For Cora had always assured her lover that, though she liked him personally, she hated men and would never marry.

Throughout the journey by train and ship Cora was wildly excited. She remembered that they 'billed and cooed like turtle doves'. It was a kind of honeymoon.

'What a pleasure to see Paris,' Cora remembered in her memoirs, 'we stayed at the Hotel de Lille et d'Albion.' (Cora changed all the names of the hotels and people – except one – in her memoirs. I will not add to the confusion.)

The next day my 'husband' took me to the top of the Arc de Triomphe; then he showed me the drains, [these were new then, and a source of civic pride to Parisians and wonder to tourists] the caves of the Panthéon and the lake full of red fish, in the Tuileries. We went to the Theatre and to Concerts. Then he took me to Meudon.

She remembered every detail of this intoxicating first visit to *la ville lumière*.

Bignell was old enough to be young Cora's father. All his

previous visits to Paris had been on business only. Now, with young Cora to teach him, he was learning to enjoy himself. It was a wonderful experience for him, for she added delight to everything by enjoying herself so much.

This holiday [Cora recounted in her memoirs] was the happiest I have had in all my life. Neither at Baden, where I spent 200,000 francs, nor in Switzerland – nowhere have I had so much fun as at Asnières and St Cloud on that visit.

Bignell took her to the famous dance hall 'Bal Mabille' where Cora, dancing the Polka with him, was immediately observed and admired. She met here a business friend of Bignell, she named 'Roubisse', a socialite pimp who brought together likely partners and organised the traffic in foreign girls for prostitution.

This was the business which had brought Bignell to Paris, and which he discussed with Roubisse while Cora was blissfully drinking her apéritif outside in the celebrated Mabille gardens.

Roubisse knew everybody and could supply every taste.

The Jardin Mabille [wrote Charles Augustus Cole in *The Imperial Paris Guide* (written for English tourists)] is tastefully laid out and illuminated. The fashionable nights are Tuesday and Saturday when the entrance is three francs. Thursday and Sunday the entrance is only two francs . . . the famed grisette is here to be found, known to every reader of a certain class of French novel. [He added, pursing his lips] A glimpse may occasionally be obtained of the 'can can', a far more expressive than elegant way of dancing, which only the presence of the police can keep within the bounds of decency.

It was Bignell's dream to make the Argyll Rooms as splendid as the Jardin Mabille.

For Cora, the greatest treat Paris could offer, however, was the Bois de Boulogne, where admiring crowds watched the Empress Eugénie taking her afternoon drive, escorted by grooms, postillions and outriders in most handsome livery. Following her came the noble ladies of her Court, in their fine carriages drawn by equally fine horses.

And following them, in the finest carriages of all, whose upholstery and fittings outshone all the rest, the most renowned courtesans of Paris flaunted their insolent beauty. Their magnificent dresses with multitudinous flounces overflowed the sides of their carriages, their exquisite jewels sparkled in the mild rays of the afternoon sun.

Money had bought all this and money ruled Paris. And money was there in abundance for those with the will and audacity to get it.

Transfixed, Cora missed nothing of the spectacle. She recognised that this was how her loving papa had foreseen her triumph. This was to be the stage on which she was to become a star. Even better, even bigger a star, because Paris was superior to London in the frank homage it paid to the great courtesans. Cora's mind was instantly made up. This was what she was determined to achieve for herself.

But the joyful holiday month of fun and pleasure was ending. Bignell announced that he could stay away from his London business no longer.

'Had Bignell declared: "It is time to die" the effect on me could not have been more disagreeable,' she remembered.

Cora replied, 'Go if you wish. I am staying here!'. She seized their passport and burned it.

'Ah,' said her lover, watching the flames consume his paper marriage, 'if I had known how this delightful holiday would end I should not have undertaken it.' 'And,' recounted Cora simply, 'he paid the hotel bill and left.'

5
Masséna

Cora was on her own again. Her goal was now clear. When she wrote her memoirs half a century later, she began:

There are women who envy our lot – our mansions – diamonds – carriages – what golden dreams!

This was exactly her own golden dream – one that Cora was determined to make come true.

Her ignorance of the Profession was profound. She had learned nothing in the Argyll Rooms because Bignell, wanting to keep Cora for himself, had shielded her from his clients. Now, with her strong practical sense, she took careful stock of herself and of her situation:

First the debit side;

1) She was plain. No denying it. By the standards of the time she was indeed plain. Her face was too round. Her complexion was too highly coloured. She had freckles. Red hair was out of fashion. Her eyes were too small. Her mouth was too big. She had a clown's face.
2) She had no lodgings – almost no money.
3) She was too young. Her body was still the body of a schoolgirl. The haughty beauties she had seen driving in the Bois were mature women. She was only fifteen years old.
4) She was a foreigner.
5) She knew no-one of influence in Paris to advise her how to get started.

But on the credit side;

1) Plain. Yes she certainly was plain. But her skin was good and her teeth absolutely perfect. And perhaps it *was* her clown's face which attracted men so much.
2) Lodgings. Anything would do to begin with. There must be plenty of cheap furnished rooms in Paris. Money – she must lay her hands on some without delay.
3) Too young. True her body was still undeveloped, but it promised to develop satisfactory curves before long, and she could count on her excellent health and vitality. She was starting her career and surely it was best to start young. Bignell had told her about the Comtesse di Castiglione, whose equipage Cora had so much admired in the Bois. This blonde Italian beauty Cavour had sent to France to spy for Italy had become the mistress of the Emperor Louis-Napoléon at sixteen.
4) A foreigner. She was indeed English by birth. But this was a positive advantage because everything English was then in high favour in Paris. English horses, English '*biftek*', Queen Victoria, English accents. She had already noticed that her anglicised pronunciation of French seemed to please male French adults just as much as it had delighted her Boulogne classmates. And Bignell had told her that most of the top Paris Courtesans were foreigners – Italian, Russian, even American.
5) Someone to advise her. Of course! She had forgotten. There was that well-spoken man-of-the-world she had met at the Mabille, Monsieur Roubisse, a friend of Bignell. She could go to see him.

Cora, young as she was, had shrewdly concluded that beauty was not enough. Even the most perfect beauty was not enough. The great courtesans must offer something more: wit, entertainment, superb food, *total luxury*. Total luxury was the lure. This needed vast amounts of money to procure and even more to maintain. Cora, with only her experience of her convent *soupe maigre*, her mother's careful 'turning the sheets economically side-to-middle', and her Grannie Watts' stringent letting down of school-dress hems, was convinced that luxury was within her imaginative power to achieve. Not sloppy bohemian luxury, but carefully planned and perfectly organised luxury. When she got her chance she would show them.

The Second Empire was all about money and how to spend it most conspicuously. New industrial enterprises, new railways, new boulevards created by the booming Stock Exchange, were founting money. The rôle of the courtesans was to mop up this flowing lava. And, to help them, Paris was full of luxury shops of every kind – wonderful jewellery, gorgeous dresses, unbelievably costly furniture, carpets, pictures and bibelots. Exquisite day and night carriages to drive in, and the finest ponies imported from England to harness to them. Not to speak of the costliest race horses. There were world-famous restaurants and staggeringly expensive food shops where the rarest titbits were imported from all over the world. Getting as much money as possible – spending as much money as possible – that was everything.

As the popular journalist of the period, Nestor Roqueplan of *Le Figaro* observed: 'Money is always chic.'

In Paris the Profession was carefully regulated: it depended on where you lived. A lady pursuing her trade in the rue de Grammont could expect to charge her 'protector' no more than 300 francs a month 'for gloves and flowers' (of course she could have several protectors).

While a lady taking up her residence in the classier rue du Helder could expect to earn 400 francs a month, plus a groom.

A lady with a residence in the rue St Lazare, or the rue de la chaussée – d'Antan could expect 500 francs a month, plus a horse and carriage.

At the top of the scale, a lady living in the Fauberg St Honoré would look no lower than a count at least for a protector (a duke would be more acceptable), who would guarantee her an allowance of 2,000 francs a month, a mansion, two carriages, two horses, a footman and a chef.

Brilliant performers could rise higher still. Lucky lorettes might skip some of the stages. In the lower ranges the competition was fearsome. The Paris police records reveal that, in 1864, there were 125,000 'immoral women' carrying on their trade of prostitution in all classes of society – of these only 30,000 were registered prostitutes.

The Goncourt brothers, close observers of the social life of the Second Empire, recorded seeing a child of eleven or so being lifted into a cab to be used for prostitution, whilst her younger sister was instructed to breathe on the cab windows so that the police should not see what was going on inside.

Cora's first adventure in Paris was with a sailor 'Aménard' – 'tender and amiable' but, unfortunately without money. Then his ship departed. Goodbye Aménard!

Cora took herself back to the Mabille in search of Monsieur Roubisse. She liked the Mabille – its steam organ, wheezing dance tunes outside in the gardens – its 5,000 gas jets lighting up the grisettes inside the dance-hall, with its scarlet damask and opulent gold-framed mirrors. You could meet absolutely everyone there.

Roubisse was willing to help. His first offering was a charming man 'Delamarche,' 'whose heart was as large as his purse was small'. Cora, however, was not seeking romance, but solvency. Goodbye Delamarche!

Now Roubisse proved really helpful. He introduced to Cora the Duc de Rivoli, Victor Masséna, grandson of Napoléon I's famous Marshal.

Masséna was in his early thirties. He was kind, courteous, affectionate, rather staid, extremely rich and generous. 'He was,' Cora wrote, 'the first link in my chain of gold.' He was unmarried, popular, lived at home with his parents, and was eager to introduce Cora to the delights the very rich enjoyed in Paris. For her part Cora was eager to learn. Their liaison lasted six years.

Upon being presented to Cora, Masséna asked her what present she would like. She answered gaily, 'A *vélocipède*'. This three-wheeled precursor of the bicycle duly arrived. Cora loved it and used it for years.

Masséna set up Cora in a fine establishment, with a renowned chef (a boisterous Southerner named Salé), servants, money to spend on clothes and jewels, and a special allowance for gambling.

Cora learned fast. Masséna and his friends were accustomed to large-scale entertaining. For weeks on end Cora received at least fifteen guests to dinner every night. Salé's bills were enormous. At first Cora dutifully checked each item with Salé, but he could not function without huge amounts of meat, poultry, fish and rare fruit at his command, and Masséna cheerfully paid the bills. Salé and Cora respected each other's strong characters, and he remained with her for many years, through good times and bad times.

Masséna encouraged Cora to go to Worth for her clothes and

there Cora made an important friend. Worth had been a counter-jumper in Bourne & Hollingsworth in Piccadilly. Now he counted the Empress Eugénie amongst his customers. He was famous in Paris as 'Monsieur Vort'.

Cora, young though she was, soon became a notable figure on the Paris scene. The gossip-columnists began to take notice and report her appearances, her clothes and her *bon mots*. Cora quickly realized the value of this publicity and encouraged it.

Trouble turned up in the shape of Masséna's wild and spoiled young nephew, Prince Achille Murat, whose claim to fame was that his grandfather had married Napoléon Bonaparte's sister, Caroline. Achille's father, Prince Lucien of Monte Corvo (Napoléon Lucien Charles Murat), had drifted to America after the fall of Napoléon. He was ineffective and foolish. He became a village postmaster and that was about all he was fit for. His wife, Caroline Georgina Frazer of Charlestown, on the other hand, was a fine, honourable woman, a descendant of George Washington's family. She supported her futile husband and horrid children by running a girl's school.

With the establishment of the Second Empire, all (even the most remote) relations of Napoléon I flocked to Paris to guzzle at the Imperial Civil List trough.

Prince Lucien was allotted 100,000 francs annually, plus two elegant residences in Paris. His wife received a similar allowance. Prince Achille Murat received an allowance of 24,000 francs annually, but was always in debt. He was ill-mannered, quarrelsome, lecherous, a drunkard, a thoroughly dissipated teenager. He was the despair of his uncle, the Emperor Louis-Napoléon, who found himself constantly called upon to pay his bills.

Prince Achille had only one accomplishment – his fine horsemanship. This is how he became friendly with Cora. One day she was enjoying herself riding her *vélocipède* on the road outside her house when he cantered by and offered to teach her to ride horseback. Cora needed no lesson. She had a naturally fine seat and handled a horse very well. Soon she went hunting with Prince Achille. She had been introduced to what was to become the deepest passion in her life – horses. Soon Prince Achille presented her with a horse of her own (no doubt the Emperor paid for this too).

Prince Achille cut across his uncle Masséna's liaison with Cora so crudely and violently that Masséna grew angry. But Cora was young and headstrong and did whatever she liked. It is about this period that a nasty brush with the police took place in Cora's happy-go-lucky life which deserves explanation.

Indulging in one of her schoolgirl pranks, Cora was riding her *vélocipède* in the street outside her house, rigged out in male fancy dress and wearing a man's wig. She was jeered at by a group of local children. Cora lost her temper and chased the children, capturing one twelve-year-old girl whom she carried off into her house.

Outside, the girls' cries for help attracted a crowd who threatened to invade Cora's house. When the police broke in they found Cora trying to force the girl to kiss the ground and apologise, which the girl refused to do.

Cora had to pay a fine of 150 francs plus 400 francs damages. No-one, apparently, upbraided the girl for jeering and mocking a stranger. She was the heroine of the encounter – Cora the villain.

When this episode in Cora's life is considered, it seems likely that the punishment Cora was trying to inflict on the girl for her rude behaviour was one she herself had learned in her Boulogne convent school days. It seems exactly a schoolgirl code of crime and punishment. And Cora never grew out of those schooldays in Boulogne. They were with her all her life.

Prince Achille, only two years older than Cora, had a very bad influence on her, to the despair of her protector Masséna, the Duc de Rivoli, who loved her. Achille was always getting himself involved in duels, passing bad cheques, causing scandals, and taking part in drunken orgies. Finally the Emperor lost patience with him, paid off his debts and sent him to Algeria to join the army of occupation. Masséna was glad to see him go. And perhaps Cora too. Achille's behaviour was not her idea of fun.

Nevertheless Cora had behaved badly to Masséna over Achille and at the close of her life regretted it. He had always behaved well to her: 'Altogether adorable and the man who received least in return,' she recorded sadly in her memoirs. He loved her. She could not love him. She was to find that she was unable to love any man.

Cora realized the time had come to regulate her life-style, for she liked order. She determined that when a liaison was finished it was finished, and she herself would terminate it. Cora's code of conduct (new in the Profession) shows how confident and fiercely independent she had already become. She always declared her code to her lovers before any new liaison, like the good businesswoman she was.

Cora's real passion was not men but horses. She became a renowned rider, and presently shared a large house (because of its commodious stables, which she soon filled with fine horses) with an Alsacian courtesan named Caroline Hassé. This lady was a large butter-blonde of meagre intelligence and very white skin, which she enhanced by using sheets and pillowslips of black silk on her vast bed. She did very well in her Profession. Some men want just that.

There was a wry postscript to Prince Achille's affair with Cora. He had grandly promised that on the day of his marriage he would honour his post-dated cheque to her for 200,000 francs: 'Eight days before the marriage,' (to Princess Salomé Dodiani, daughter of Prince Nicholas Davidovitch of Mingrelia, Russia), Cora recounted in her memoirs, 'I tore up the cheque and returned it to him with my good wishes.' He would not have honoured it anyway.

For six years Masséna continued to keep Cora in the style to which he had accustomed her. And Cora's passion for horses increased. Even after they parted they remained friends. He still cared for her and worried over the future of his schoolgirl protégée he had unwittingly transformed into an expensive courtesan, one of the leaders of the Profession. He had taught her to spend money like water. He had taught her to gamble. He had not taught her to put something by for he himself had no experience of want. He, however, gave her a little property at Maisons Lafitte which she could sell in emergency.

Six years is a long time in the life of a young girl. What had Cora learned? She had learned how totally dependent were the very rich on those who supplied their luxuries, and especially on those who supplied their entertainment, for like small children they quickly tired of every new distraction.

They lived in each other's pockets, meeting continually, gossiping about each other continually, attending balls and banquets continually, dining and exchanging mistresses and lovers continually, relieving their boredom by inventing scandals continually. Gambling was their chief seasonal distraction. Masséna had taken Cora to Baden or Vichy every Season. Here the same group of wealthy socialites were joined by similar groups from all the capitals of Europe, including many royalties.

To while away the time not actually spent at the gaming tables there were fêtes, balls, charades, endless dinner-parties, and non-stop entertaining. Cora's unflagging energy and inexhaustible supply of practical jokes made her extremely popular.

In their suite at the Hôtel Cheval-Blanc, Vichy, Cora recalled, she and Masséna kept open house. It was always crowded with friends, friends of friends and others no-one knew at all. They just dropped in (sometimes through the window). They sang and danced and feasted and drank from morning till past midnight. The bills for food and drink were astronomical.

To understand the price of things you need to know the value of money. I was totally ignorant. The big industrialists, those Princes of Finance, should have educated me.

[Cora had to learn the hard way] At Monte Carlo I only played [the tables] once. I had brought with me 30,000 francs to pay various debts. At the Casino I was playing very carefully. I won very little. I was going very cautiously. Giulia Barucci called me a *'pintade mouilée'* [stuck up]. So I began to stake more boldly. Before long I had lost 67,000 francs.

Masséna had gone back to Paris ahead of Cora. She now had no money to pay the various tradesmen who, from being very polite and deferential (when Masséna was with her), now showed themselves to be pitiless. (They were, for the record, all paid eventually.) But, for the moment, she had no money at all. And she owed 700 francs for her hotel bill. She had to leave her luggage and belongings with the proprietor. 'How to get back to Paris, alone and penniless? I had to borrow 500 francs from the hotel cash-register. Since I was broke I had to travel like poor people travel. No occasion to blush, yet that same season during my visit I had been entertained by and had entertained the very greatest ladies.'

It was during her last visit to Baden in 1869, an ominous year, that Cora's gentlemen friends played their most successful practical joke. They had all made holes in their pockets through which they dropped exploding firecrackers in the gaming rooms. The gamblers and croupiers were terrified. Where could these diabolic new war weapons be coming from?

William, Prince of Orange, heir to the throne of Holland became Cora's next protector, the second link in her chain of gold. He was a weak nervous blond, a bore, totally out of sympathy with the country he was destined to rule. He only cared about the pleasures of Paris and tried his best to be a *boulevardier*. Cora nicknamed him 'Duc Citron'. When he reluctantly returned to Holland he gave Cora a magnificent pearl necklace. She had found him heavy going.

6
Morny

Cora had learned a lot about men, rich men, by now – what they wanted and what they thought they wanted. It was the chase they enjoyed more than the kill. Since no one man was ever to 'own' her, they were ready to ruin themselves in pursuit of her. Especially as she was such fun to chase.

Cora declared in her memoirs:

A handsome well-mannered young man, who has offered me his arm, his love and his money, has every right to believe and to declare himself indeed 'my true lover' – that is to say my lover for an hour, my escort for a month, my friend for ever . . . that is how I understand the business. My temperament does not lend itself to uncontrollable passion . . . I can claim that I have never had an 'amant de coeur'.

How can one translate that? What Cora meant was 'one true lasting love for one man and one man only.' Of course that is exactly what she did have. The *one*, the only man in Cora's man-besieged life, was her father, defaulting Professor Crouch.

As to what it is customary to describe as 'blind passion', 'fatal allurement'. NO! I have never known these emotions. And so much the better for my peace of mind . . . I have known women wreck their lives on such illusions . . .

Such determination left Cora free to become a truly professional 'Professional', applying herself to this task with all her immense energy and gaiety, combined with her passion for order and housewifely cleanliness.

Beauty, Cora had learned, is a concept which changes from season to season. Cora knew she was plain. But many men swore she was a beauty. She behaved like a beauty, with the assured grace of reigning beauties. Even better, Cora's lively temperament animated her clown's face at all times with a radiance which banished boredom and swept men off their feet.

In the stock-exchange Second Empire a mistress was valued according to what she cost. The more extravagant the mistress, the more devoted her lover. Cora became a most enthusiastic spender – on her person, her stables, her mansions crammed with pictures, sculpture, precious books in rare bindings, costly bibelots, and on her lavish entertainment, not to mention her gorgeous gowns and jewels.

What we now describe as 'titillation' had nothing to do with Cora's success. There was nothing which the sated wealthy satyrs of the Second Empire had not already tried *ad nauseum*. Any reasonably agile woman (or man) could learn the gymnastics of the entire *Kama Sutra*, and, since this was equally available to the suburbs, the pleasure-sated top society of Louis-Napoléon's Paris had no time for it.

Paris top society was always after something new, more expensive, more luxurious, still harder to get. And Cora enjoyed providing it for them, for she was a born innovator.

Red hair was out of fashion – Cora brought it back. Hair dye was unknown in Paris – Cora introduced it. Cosmetics were secret – Cora flaunted them. No Parisienne had altered her eyelashes before – Cora tinted hers.

She sent to London for all her dyes, tints, paints and powders, introducing 'slap', that popular dolly-mop mixture of bismuth and ochre, into the most expensive Paris salons. She experimented all the time – a new complexion every day, a new look every evening. Her complexion varied from 'silver' to 'pearl', from 'snowy' to 'milk white' to 'sunset'. The red of her curls varied in tone each evening, even to blue and purple. She introduced wigs and coils of false hair into her toilette.

All these aids to beauty were recorded with delight in the gossip columns and were bitterly denounced not only by 'respectable' women but also by her sisters in the Profession.

When Cora's countryman Worth, the famous English couturier

of the rue de la Paix, wanted to introduce a new style, he turned to Cora for help and she never disappointed him.

Towards the end of the 1860s Worth was heartily tired of the crinoline. But the empress Eugénie (whose evening crinoline dresses he had made in fairy-tale gossamer tulles, delicate silks and rare lace) would not change from this style. So Worth turned to Cora, and she launched Worth's epoch-making bustle. Cora had the perfect figure for the bustle, the panache to carry it off, and was quite ready to take on the Empress.

Paris never forgot the famous occasion when the Empress Eugénie, attired in regal splendour, glittering with jewels and orders, honoured the Italian Opera with the Emperor in full regalia, attended by their *cent-gardes*. The crowded audience had already turned in homage towards the royal box when Cora arrived in the opposite box, gorgeously dressed and bejewelled, marvellously made up. With one accord the audience turned towards Cora's box to stare in admiration. The Empress was outraged. Her gracious smile snapped off. She stormed out of the royal box in fury, forcing the Emperor to accompany her. She should have known better. Paris never forgot this imperial display of temper. They told each other that Cora Pearl would have handled the situation better and that it was the Empress Eugénie who had behaved like an upstart.

Cora's resounding success in her chosen *métier* upset the ladies of Paris, both those of the Profession and the legal wives. They could never understand how this plain young Englishwoman, apparently without trying, enticed their lovers, husbands and sons, besides vast sums of money, away from them.

Dark stories circulated of drugs and love philtres. Jealous lorettes started spiteful rumours that Cora was bowlegged, drank heavily, was a lesbian and daughter of a low ostler, and so on.

Horse-riding, in which Cora excelled, had become important in Paris. The courtesans and the noble ladies of the court were obliged to ride. But it was not a sport they cared for. Fine carriages and liveries gave more scope for display. Horses, they sneered, were an English obsession. But then everything English was in fashion.

Cora's only rival in this field was, briefly, another English courtesan, 'Skittles' – an illiterate blonde pocket venus from the stews of Liverpool. She could not speak a word of French. She was not yet twenty-three and had come to Paris to try her luck. She did not need to earn money. Her financial future was already assured because 'Harry tarry' (Lord Hartington), whose mistress she had been for a few months, had settled a £2,000 annuity on her for life (a considerable amount of money in those days), besides a fine Mayfair mansion and a string of ponies. In addition, Hartington's father, the Duke of Devonshire, added a large *douceur* in compensation for the damage to her pride on the break-up of the affair. So money was not what Skittles was after. She liked the game for itself.

In Paris Skittles immediately became the mistress of Achille Fould, financial adviser to the Emperor and an extremely wealthy old Jewish banker. Fould gave Skittles sound advice on how to succeed and what to avoid in the maelstrom of Paris society. Skittles soon made the gossip columns. 'What perfect taste! What elegance! What grace on horse-back . . .' purred Count Albert de Maugny.

But Skittles was too rooted in England, and she never became one of the leading courtesans of Paris. She drifted towards the English diplomatic colony where shy youths were more in her line, had a devastating love affair with young Wildred Blunt, and returned to England for good.

Skittles was class-conscious and 'knew her place': when she persuaded the master of the famous English Fox-Hunt 'The Quorn' to let her join them, she followed the hunt at the rear so as not to offend the aristocratic wives, though she rode so much better than they did. This was something Cora would never have accepted.

Cora was friendly with one of the leading Paris courtesans, stupid and illiterate but kind and beautiful Giulia Barucci, who had made a great fortune in the Profession, though still very young. Barucci loved the military (any rank) but loved the Virgin Mary even more, being deeply religious. She kept a statue of the Madonna beside her stupendous bed (which she good-naturedly lent to society ladies, sometimes, to help them conduct their clandestine love affairs).

Barucci remained loyal to her native Italian village. She made it a practice, after wearing them once, to give all her most sumptuous dresses to her sister to take back to this village to dress up the statue of the Madonna in the village church.

Barucci was consumptive and died in her twenties, but not before she had greatly intrigued Edward, Prince of Wales, who specially asked to meet her when visiting Paris.

The Duc de Gramont-Caderousse (also young and consumptive

and a friend of Prince Edward), arranged the meeting. Barucci, who had little concept of time, arrived extremely late, wearing nothing at all except a transparent gauze shift. This she presently lifted with her most appealing smile and, turning round, showed the Prince her plump ivory arse. 'The best thing I've got,' she explained graciously.

One bright afternoon in December, with the temperature four degrees below zero, Cora, wrapped in expensive furs, was enjoying herself skating on the frozen lake in the Bois de Boulogne. A tall elegantly dressed gentleman with waxed moustache and imperial, driving by in his Chinese sleigh, called out teasingly: 'Cora on ice! What a paradox!'

It was the Duc de Morny, half-brother to the Emperor, whose *coup d'état* he had masterminded. Morny was a powerful politician, a leading financier, Chief Minister of State and much else besides. He had had his roving eye on Cora for some time. Cora called back gaily: 'Well now that the ice is broken do take me for a drink!'

Thus began the most interesting of Cora's liaisons. Morny was wealthy, highly intelligent, witty, handsome, with perfect manners and no scruples. Like Cora he had no time for pomposity. He loved the company of writers, artists, musicians and people of the theatre. He had enjoyed the favours of many women and much preferred the entertainers to the nobly born.

When he had been sent to Moscow as French Ambassador, he played the rôle in the grandest style. He quite improperly used the diplomatic bag to send trainloads of Russian valuables, duty-free, to Paris where they were auctioned on his behalf, for 800,000 roubles.

Morny also profited by the social life of Moscow to meet and marry Princess Sophy Trubetskoi, illegitimate daughter of the Czar, and very rich. Princess Sophy, tiny in stature, was a famous beauty. Her skin was of porcelain whiteness – her masses of hair, pale gold, and her eyes jet black. They made a striking pair at imperial balls, and there were no scandals. Morny conducted his extramarital affairs with diplomatic discretion – Princess Sophy biding her time without acrimony.

On his way up, to help his many successful speculations, Morny had used the fortune of the Countess le Hon, wife of the Belgian Ambassador, and was the father of her illegitimate daughter.

Charles Auguste, Duc de Morny, had distinguished ancestors,

from whom he had inherited his good looks, intelligence, and genius for political manoeuvring. The great Talleyrand's illegitimate son, Count Flahaut [1], was his father. Morny, in turn, was the Count's illegitimate son by his mistress Queen Hortense of Holland, the daughter of the Empress Josephine by her first marriage to Beauharnais: a remarkable ancestry and nearly all from the wrong side of the blanket.

Significantly, Morny chose as his insignia a hortensia (his mother's name) surmounted by a crown, which he had painted on his carriages. Morny loved to embarrass Louis-Napoléon and the Empress Eugénie at court balls in the Tuileries, by declaring, with a charming gesture:

Ici, nous sommes tous bâtards!
I am [he explained] a very complicated person. I am the son of a queen, the brother of an Emperor and the son-in-law of another Emperor – and all of us are illegitimate!

It was Morny's delight, dressed like Richelieu in a robe of violet velvet, to play Chopin to Cora on the grand piano in his private salon in his official office – or read poetry to her from his favourite poet, de Musset – or rattle out the frivolous songs his friend Offenbach was then composing.

Morny had himself written, under a pseudonym, a successful one-act operetta for Offenbach's Bouffes Théâtre entitled *Monsieur Choufleury restera chez lui*.

Morny's friends suited Cora perfectly. She was now in a world with which she was familiar, and the fun Morny and their friends enjoyed together was very much to her taste.

Morny, significantly, was old enough to be Cora's father, an age gap which recurred in all Cora's major liaisons.

Morny had loved many women from all classes. He cared deeply for the theatre and had helped at least two famous actresses to get started. There was Rachel, a starveling Jewish girl he discovered singing in the Paris Streets. Her father was a poor peddler. Rachel's voice, naturally deep and sonorous, attracted Morny's attention. He introduced her to the Comédie Française where she received an excellent training. Her talent soon proved itself in classic Greek

---

[1] Comte de Flahaut de la Billarderie, later to become French Ambassador to London, through the influence of Talleyrand.

tragedies, especially *Phèdre*, in which she became world famous. She died of tuberculosis before she was thirty.

The other successful actress Morny launched was red-haired Sarah Bernhardt. Her father was a lawyer and her mother was briefly Morny's mistress. It was Morny who arranged for the bastard child's education at the conservatoire, and introduced her to the Comédie Française where she made her début before she was eighteen, four years after Rachel's death.

The two permanent passions in Morny's life were horses and the theatre. His first present to Cora was a superb white Arab mare. He was surprised how well she rode, for she assured him she had never had a riding lesson in her life.

Cora by now had realized her dream and bought a charming country house (really a little château) near Olivet, about four miles from Orléans. It had fine stables and was Cora's joy and pride. She furnished her beloved 'Beauséjour' lavishly. Her Axminster and Wilton carpets were specially woven for her and sent over from England. Casts of her beautiful hands in silver, bronze and gold were strewn on her mirror-polished little occasional tables. Her superb bathroom (a must for all top courtesans) displayed a superb bronze bath, cast for her by Chevalier of Paris, engraved in gold with her monogram. Her stained glass windows displayed the Virgil motto:

> *Parcere subjectis et deballare superbos*
> Spare the Humble. Attack the Proud!

Not, you might think, altogether appropriate for a courtesan whose income depended on the proud and mighty. But it was right for Cora.

At this period there were revolutionary movements bubbling all over Europe, political movements and also feminist movements. Cora showed no interest whatsoever. She was a movement on her own, one might say.

There was a lot of brass about in Beauséjour, including many stair-rods which Cora's maids had to keep polished to mirror brightness. There was always much scrubbing of parquet and buffing of mahogany to bring her floors and furniture up to Cora's exacting standards. And outside her front door was a mat, sternly commanding visitors to wipe their feet.

Every weekend Cora received a host of assorted guests. The *Jour de l'an* was a particular holiday at Beauséjour when all her guests brought Cora presents. These ranged from *marrons glacés*, each wrapped in a 1,000-franc banknote, to a small live piglet, which Cora named Emmanuel, and whose ears and tail her guests painted bright green with carpenter's paint left over from work on the window shutters.

Beauséjour had pretty wooded grounds on the banks of the river Loire. The estate included four and a half hectares of land, also heavy mortgages as well, which Cora never managed to pay off. The depredations of three wars (the Franco–Prussian War, the First World War and the Second World War), have taken their toll of Beauséjour, and invading German troops carried off most of the furniture and fittings as well as pictures and bibelots. But up to 1949 at least, the château itself was still there, and old men in the village remembered Cora and what fun was always going on there. The not-so-old remembered tales their fathers had told them of Cora tossing a gold twenty-franc Louis coin out of the window for them to fetch wine from the local wineshop and how she always told them to keep the change.

This sort of country life (unlike Louis Napoléon's pompous country parties at Compiègne, which cost so much and produced nothing but ennui), the Duc de Morny loved, and he was always a welcome guest at Beauséjour.

Morny and Cora were clearly good for each other. In her memoirs Cora wrote:

He was a perfect gentleman. No-one could offer a compliment more gracefully, and his compliments were never commonplace. He had a horror of banality. He even made it pleasant when he felt obliged to reproach me. He was one of those people who never age and linger in one's memory always so alive. It was always my pleasure to listen to him – his wit and his fine critical comments. And always a joy to hear him play the piano and sing little songs.

Morny helped Cora in another way too, which she never forgot. She had arrived one season at Baden with much baggage, much money, a wagon full of suitcases, six horses and all her staff including the indispensable Salé. Cora, dressed in her newest Worth creation, took herself to the Casino to dine and gamble.

At the entrance to the gaming rooms the Commissionaire stopped me from entering. It seems I was the subject of a special interdiction from on high. I wondered what possible motive singled me out for exclusion [could it have been the scandal of the exploding firecrackers?] and prevented me from losing my money at the tables like any humble Marchioness?

I was told 'by order of the Queen'. I returned to my friends in the dining room and told them what had happened. They couldn't believe me. As we were talking a servant came up to me with a card.

'Hurry up and finish your dinner. I will take you in on my arm.' Morny.

Dinner was soon over. I made my way into the gaming rooms on Morny's arm between two banks of curious onlookers.

Morny had been to see the Queen. (In Morny's stables he kept 110 fine horses as well as a special racing stable of over 40 racehorses, cared for by a staff of English grooms.) Great was Morny's joy and great was Cora's delight when Morny's favourite racehorse 'Perle' (named in honour of Cora), won the autumn *Cézarewitch* for him in 1864.

It was the culmination of their liaison. For years Morny had been wearing himself out burning the candle at both ends. He died aged only fifty-three, probably as a result of overdosing himself with arsenic-based rejuvenation tablets.

His wife, Sophy, with a fine Slavic gesture, cut off her mane of pale gold hair and cast it into his grave at his funeral. Then a year later she quietly married her lover of long standing, the Duke of Sesto, a Spanish grandee who had once been engaged to the Senorita de Montijo who had become the Empress Eugénie . . . a small world.

As for the Empress, immediately she heard of Morny's death she had all his personal papers removed. Did her secretaries find the cabinet Morny kept by his bedside? It contained photographs of every one of his mistresses in the nude (no doubt taken by Nadar, the famous photographer) – Morny had each photograph prettily painted with flowers.

There must have been much anxiety in the Coulisses of the Tuileries and much teeth-grinding elsewhere – for the possibilities of scandal and blackmail were awesome. As to Cora, she certainly would not have minded. She had a splendid body of which she was justly proud.

7
Friends and Enemies

Essential to Cora's household, balancing her exuberant extravagant chef, Salé, was her faithful housekeeper – Madame Eugénie Laforêt. This devoted woman stayed with Cora through good times and bad times and catastrophic times, paid or unpaid, well or ill, until Cora died. Lacqueys, housemaids, laundresses and parlour-maids came and went over the years. Madame Laforêt stayed.

When I read the spiteful and cruel rubbish written about Cora Pearl, I ask myself how such a vulgar, cruel fiend as they try to make Cora out to have been could possibly have kept the loyalty and affection of Salé and Madame Laforêt over the many years they were together. And I prefer to trust the servants, not the gossip-mongers.

A good few years older than Cora, Madame Laforêt had once been in the Profession herself. She must have known something about men. What she knew for certain was a star when she saw one. Cora was that star. Like the dresser without whom the great actress cannot go on stage, Madame Laforêt had her role to play – and Cora had complete confidence in her.

Madame Laforêt was the perfect foil for Cora; thin, quiet, devoted, immensely discreet, always dressed in black with a neat white crochet collar and a small white cap like a meringue. She was Cora's best friend and Cora talked over with her every difficult situation in her often rowdy life, and sometimes even took her advice.

Their relationship was one of mutual trust, not at all mistress and servant. Ladylike, Madame Laforêt with her quiet well-bred voice, never raised, organised Cora's household smoothly – the continual dinner parties where every detail had to be perfect, the *travesti* balls which no-one but Cora could have conceived and no-one but Madame Laforêt master-minded. The succession of protectors, some whose reign was very brief, others who lasted for years – all looked up to and confided in trustworthy Madame Laforêt.

Wherever Cora was, there was life and there was fun. Salé and Madame Laforêt relished the fun and enjoyed their essential rôles in Cora's success.

As the years scurried by, Madame Laforêt began to suffer from arthritis which distressed Cora, who was herself so vigorously healthy. Who could guess that the housekeeper would outlive her mistress?

Cora's luxurious dinner-parties were the talk of Paris. She was always dreaming up costly surprises to dazzle her guests. She remembered these with pride at the end of her life – for instance the rarest out-of-season fruits served on a dewy bed of wildly extravagant out-of-season Parma violets.

From time to time during the season, Cora gave large parties to which she invited the wives as well as their husbands. This was something new and disquieting in the Paris social set-up, for Cora's male guests included clients from the Tuileries Court circles. But Cora had no time for hypocrisy.

Usually the wives did not accept Cora's invitations, but one or two highly-placed socialites accepted out of curiosity, including the beautiful Comtesse Louise de Mercy d'Argenteau, the Duchesse de Cadore and Princess Pauline Von Metternich, wife of the Austrian Ambassador.

Princess Metternich was small, restless, and full of curiosity about the lives of Paris harlots. As she said of herself, she had the face of a monkey and a monkey's inquisitiveness. To relieve the boredom of court life Princess Metternich slipped out on to the Grand Boulevards one night, unescorted, wrapped in a cloak, its hood concealing her face.

Very soon she was stopped by an angry gendarme who brusquely demanded to see her prostitute's licence, whereupon the Princess drew aside her hood and revealed her face. The gendarme, when he had recovered his breath, earnestly implored her to return home at once.

What Princess Metternich and her adventurous high society friends were most anxious to see in Cora's mansion, of course, was her bathroom. The imagination of great ladies, no less than suburban housewives, can be torrid. No doubt they had heard of Skittles' famous water-closet with its celebrated swansdown seat, in her luxurious Mayfair residence, long since gone under the hammer. No doubt they expected Cora to have something even more exotic.

Princess Metternich and her inquisitive friends were sadly disappointed and the Comtesse later described Cora's bathroom as 'neither refined, nor complete' – a sad set-back when she 'had been expecting so much'.

These nosey-parker ladies would have done much better to have inspected the bathroom of the Countess Païva in her *nouveau-riche* Palace on the Champs-Elysées. But Païva did not invite ladies, nor could they have accepted if she had. Her reputation was too shady. Nevertheless, in money-mad Paris of the Second Empire unlimited amounts of money ensured respect. Only Paris, at that hectic period, could have fostered Païva. Her history is illuminating.

Païva, born in the Moscow ghetto in 1819, was the illegitimate daughter of the Russian Grand Duke Constantine and the pretty young wife of a poor Jewish tailor named Lachmann. They named her Thérèse.

When Thérèse was still a very small girl her mother contracted smallpox and was promptly abandoned by her Grand Duke. In despair over her lost looks her mother covered all the mirrors in the house with black crêpe. Thérèse was married off at the age of seventeen to an indigent Jewish tailor by whom she had a son. Two years later she abandoned her husband and child and fled to Paris to seek her fortune. She became the mistress of the famous pianist Henry Hertz, who gave her an entrée to the exciting world of arts and letters. But when Hertz took her to a reception at the Tuileries she was not allowed in. This set-back gave Thérèse the passionate desire for revenge which dominated her life and it was said, not without reason, fuelled the Franco–Prussian war and the cata-strophic defeat of the French.

In 1848 Thérèse, deciding she needed a title, abandoned Hertz, equipped herself with a costly trousseau, on tic, and ensnared a Portuguese nobleman whom she married in 1851 (her Jewish tailor husband having obligingly died in 1849). Now legitimately entitled to call herself the 'Condesa Albino-Francisco de Païva Aranjo', she abandoned her noble Portuguese husband after the wedding night, keeping his title, and took up with the Prussian multi-millionaire Count Guido von Donnersmarck, eleven years her junior, whose income never fell below three million francs a year.

Thérèse now began to realize all her dreams of self-glorification and revenge. She chose the Champs-Elyseés as the proper site for her Hollywood-style dream palace. It took ten years to build and was finished only four years before the Franco–Prussian War.

The 'Hotel Païva', as it was always known, was the talk of Paris. The salon was hung with crimson damask specially woven for her in Lyons at a cost of 800,000 francs. The ceiling, painted by Baudry, depicted night being chased away by Aurora the dawn.

The Hollywood-style grand staircase was built of solid onyx. Païva's bathroom was of marble, her bath of onyx, the taps of gilded bronze set with precious stones. The bathroom ceiling – also painted by Baudry – cost 100,000 francs. Païva's great bed was carved from precious woods inset with ivory. On one side of this bed was a large safe where she kept her jewels.

The statuary, carved specially for her by the most famous sculptors in Paris, were, in the Russian style, much too big, but not too big for Païva's self-glorification. Païva was icy. She could only live in freezing rooms and no fire was ever permitted in her grandiose grates.

Cora always hated this inhuman woman, totally dedicated to money, and who (now approaching fifty years of age) considered herself the doyenne of the Paris courtesans, being the richest, and therefore entitled to set standards for the rest. Païva disapproved of Cora, whose life-style was so different from her own, and Cora believed that Païva was a spy.

In fact Païva had no friends. She needed none. She hated dogs. She hated cats. She hated children. She was harsh to her terrified servants. She fired her gardeners if she spotted a fallen leaf on her immaculate lawns. She employed one old man, in her great country château, whose job it was to close all the heavy shutters of the 300 windows each night and open them all again each morning. The job killed him.

Her 'salons', for distinguished men only, were uneasy, notwithstanding the opulent food and overwhelming décor. Païva kept writing-material handy, requesting famous poets to write a sonnet about her onyx staircase or Baudry's lush ceilings. She always had to squeeze something out of her guests.

Cora was right. Païva and her Prussian protector were indeed spying for Prussia. Like a bad Hollywood melodrama, Païva was plotting to revenge herself on France for that old snub at the entry to the Tuileries reception. She had to wait nearly fifty years for her revenge.

A lover Cora remembered with particular affection was Khalil Bey – a Turkish Pasha of immense wealth and beautiful manners. 'An imperturbable gambler, a delightful host,' Cora enjoyed his 'Oriental Palace' in the best part of Paris, where 'enjoying his oriental hangings, rare perfumes, soft divans and luxurious marble baths,' she felt, she declared, 'inside the Arabian nights.'

On one occasion he found Cora in his salon playing with a box of exquisitely carved ivory skittles. He said nothing but, on her arrival home, there was the box of skittles waiting for her. Cora wrote him a charming letter of thanks in her seemly Jane Austen prose, in the flowing orthography learned at her Boulogne convent school. Later she prudently had her present valued – 4,500 francs.

But even Khalil Bey's immense fortune could not keep pace with his Paris life-style – his exotic banquets for Prince Edward, Cora and 'La bande', and their lovers and assorted visiting royalties. So one day he left for Turkey 'to make another fortune' and never returned.

Appreciative of good manners and courtesy, Cora never tolerated boorish behaviour no matter how high-ranking the source. Prince Demidoff had no charms except his vast wealth. He liked to annoy Cora in public by keeping on his hat in her presence.

One day, at the famous Maison Dorée restaurant, Cora requested Prince Demidoff to remove his hat. He refused. Cora raised the elegant cane she was carrying and smashed his hat on his head. The Manager hurried on to the scene to stop the trouble before the police arrived. All Cora said afterwards was that she was sorry, not for hurting Demidoff but for breaking her cane, which was a very handsome one.

Morny's sudden death deprived Cora of the pleasure she had planned to give him, in the form of a particularly personal golden goblet. It had been modelled and cast by their mutual friend

Gustave Doré – in the form of Cora's superb breasts, her lovely clasping hands forming the base. Gustave Doré was just finishing the gold casting when Morny died.

Morny's death, which was disastrous for the Emperor who now had no-one to advise him but his wife Eugénie, brought all Morny's friends – the musicians and the artists he preferred – closer together. These were not the mediocrities favoured by the Tuileries and the official Salon, who fêted chocolate-cream Winterhalter, ignored Courbet and Manet, passed over Renoir and left Monet to starve. Writers too had to watch their step – Flaubert was a friend of Morny but the Emperor did nothing to stop *Madame Bovary* being prosecuted.

Their grief over Morny's death brought Cora and Gustave Doré closer together. They had much in common and they became lovers. Doré was a phenomenal artist, brilliant in every branch of art except the one in which he craved to excel – vast 'historic' paintings. His wood-engravings (illustrating the Bible, Shakespeare, Rabelais, Cervantes and Dante, to name but a few) made him world-famous and rich. His pictures of the East End of London are still breathtaking. He was also a romantic sculptor in the grand manner.

Doré loved England which in turn liked his work and liked him, and (accolade) Queen Victoria herself smiled on him, because Albert liked his romantic engravings, and she invited him to Windsor.

Cora and Doré got on so well together that they contemplated marriage. Doré was small, slim, rosy-cheeked and blond. He looked like a schoolboy, and continued to look like a schoolboy all his life. Apart from his non-stop energy for work he possessed another talent which endeared him to athletic Cora – a physical agility which could have assured him a livelihood in any first-class circus. Doré walked on his hands as easily as on his feet. Somersaulting forwards and backwards came naturally to him. He terrified his friends by walking on his hands along narrow unprotected outside parapets many storeys high, and then returning the same way.

He only needed three hours sleep a night and put much planning and joy into his famous studio parties which Cora (herself an expert on entertaining) greatly relished. At Doré's parties you would meet Rossini, George Sand, the irrepressible quadroon novelist Dumas

père, dancers of the can-can from the Varietés, Doré's special friend
Offenbach ('the Mozart of the Boulevards') for whose saucy little
Théâtre Bouffes Doré designed and painted scenery and costumes,
the gay Bouffes circle of writers, singers and dancers, the dazzling
Hortense Schneider, and the liveliest of Cora's *bande*.

At these studio parties, which Morny had so much enjoyed, the
food was always delicious, the surprises astonishing, the *travestis*
hilarious, the practical jokes non-stop. There was fencing and
boxing and comic acrobatics, and Doré's adored pug dogs enjoying
the fun. Presiding over all loomed Doré's mother, in a black lace
mantilla, or 'moorish' robes surmounted by a large turban –
insisting on devoting her life to her talented son.

Somewhere along the line Cora had a very brief affair, (probably
what she herself described as 'my lover for an hour') with the
bohemian wealthy young Duc de Gramont Caderousse, friend of
the Prince of Wales. Although dying of tuberculosis, he was a great
practical joker; it was the only occupation he ever took seriously. (I
think he must have been someone like a young Spike Milligan.) He
was half-insane, immensely popular, and dead before he was thirty.

The real love of Gramont Caderousse's life was Hortense
Schneider, discovered and launched by Offenbach. She had quickly
become a famous star. The Duc's last Easter present to her was a
giant Easter egg containing an elegant full-size phaeton, complete
with well-bred pony and smart English groom.

Prince Edward adored Paris, where he was better known and
more popular than in England, where Queen Victoria resolutely
kept him out of the limelight. Prince Edward admired Hortense
Schneider and haunted her theatre dressing room. When she was on
stage singing he could be seen happily walking her eight little dogs
along the boulevard.

8
Plon-Plon

Celebrities attract gossip. Outrageous celebrities attract outrageous gossip, and Cora was soon affectionately known as 'the queen of outrage'. Alert to the value of publicity as any twentieth-century film starlet, Cora had courted publicity at the start of her career. Now publicity not only courted but pursued her.

Cora was one of those rare women who enjoy telling a story against themselves. For instance there was that handsome Serbian prince in the splendid trappings of an officer in the Serbian army, 'a perfect gentleman in every way' and a gallant lover. He hinted at some family trouble which had exiled him to Paris, and professed the utmost contempt for money. Cora and he went everywhere together – country walks, rides in the Bois, little *tête-à-tête* dinners, etc. He reminded Cora, she confesses in her memoirs, of her teenage days with Bignell when she first fell in love with Paris.

It was customary in the Profession, for a new lover to offer a valuable initial present and a handsome lump sum of money at the end of the affair. Carried away for once, Cora did not insist on her rule – 'no money, no favours'. The gallant Prince de Hersant was her guest for fifteen days. On the sixteenth day he disappeared. So did a valuable diamond brooch Prince Napoléon had given her. He was, Cora declared: 'A second-hand soldier and Prince of Rogues.' It served her right for breaking her own rules. But she bore no malice. It made a good story and she took care never to break her own rule again.

Another story concerns a visiting prince (this time a real prince) who having seen Cora queening it at a dinner party, immediately sent her his card on which he had inscribed simply:

ou? – quand? – combien?

The lady returned the card at once with her reply:

Ce Soir – chez moi – pour rien.

This seems probable except that Cora was now very strict about keeping her own rules of which number one was NO MONEY – NO FAVOURS.

No it certainly wasn't Cora. It was in fact the great tragic actress Rachel and the Prince was – but why should I tell you? You must find out for yourself.

The following Cora story is certainly true:

A middle-aged bureaucrat of some importance was eager to enjoy Cora's favours. But he was so afraid of it becoming known that he guarded his visit with every conceivable 'cover up'. Cora, whose lovers included far more important civil servants and whose ideal one was the Duc de Morny, who did not care a fig for public opinion, decided to teach the cowardly bureaucrat a lesson.

Her timorous client arrived, anxiously peering to left and right to be sure no-one was watching. No man, certainly no middle-aged civil servant, looks his best without his trousers. Just as her client took his off, the door of Cora's bedroom burst open and a crowd of her friends pushed their way into the room. The wretched man seized his trousers and escaped as fast as he could. Soon afterwards, however, the Chief of Police arrived, threatening Cora with deportation for daring to insult a highly-placed government official.

Cora loathed hypocrisy and knew too much of what went on in government to have any respect for its ministers, however important and powerful, if they did not behave like gentlemen. This was not Cora's first brush with French law, but she had yet to learn just how powerful it was and how ruthless its police.

Now this story is also certainly true. It was repeated far and wide – some versions locating the event in Beauséjour others in her Paris mansion in the rue de Chaillot, or in different famous Paris restaurants – but in fact it took place in the Café Riche.

Needing a rich client, Cora was entertaining a party of wealthy socialites (all male of course) to dinner one night at the famous Café

Riche. The wines were impeccable. The food was delicious. The conversation sparkling.

Cora proposed a wager: she would produce a dish her guests would be unable to eat. Bets were made and *louis d'or* showered on the dining-table. Cora withdrew to order this strange *plat*, which soon arrived in the shape of an enormous, covered silver serving dish, borne by two sturdy waiters, preceded by the chef, and heralded by a trumpet call. The chef, with a flourish, whipped off the silver cover to reveal Cora, naked as Eve before the fall, curled up like a whiting, on a bed of flowers. The chef proceeded to sprinkle Cora with sprigs of parsley. Cora had won her bet.

This was typical of Cora's life style, combining her love of practical jokes, gambling, and circus knock-about. Other famous Paris courtesans might have exposed their glamorous nudity at a private male party. But only Cora would have added the finishing touch of sprinkling parsley.

Cora was by now at the top of her profession. Her expenditure was phenomenal, always exceeding her income. It was time for her to take a new protector. Her new protector was to be Prince Napoléon. He fancied talented women with slum backgrounds (bottle-washers or street singers). Cora's background was far from that. She was a new experience for him. Prince Napoléon was twenty-two years older than Cora; a father-daughter 'incest' situation which seemed to appeal to them both. Their liaison lasted for a decade.

Napoléon Joseph Charles Paul Bonaparte – Prince Napoléon, 'Plon-Plon' to his intimates, was by all accounts detestable. He was bad-tempered, ill-mannered, foul-tongued, extremely jealous and consumed with envy for his cousin, the Emperor Napoléon III, whom he considered in every way inferior to himself.

His annual income, allotted to him by the Emperor from the Civil List, was a million francs. He had built for himself a show-piece mansion on the Champs-Elysées, the Villa Diomède, or Palais Pompeien, an exact copy of a Roman Villa in Pompei. Besides this, he owned the great country estate of Meudon, which Cora had first glimpsed with Bignell, with its forests and hunting, as well as an apartment in the Palais Royale, where he kept his wife, pious little Princess Clothilde, daughter of King Victor Emmanuel of Italy, and their children.

Plon-Plon, in profile, somewhat resembled the first Napoléon, which the Emperor Napoleon III did not. Plon-Plon had been described by the Archduke Maximilian as 'Looking like a second-rate basso in a second-class Italian operatic company.'

He was well educated, interested in modern technology, especially electricity, and fancied himself as a connoisseur of the Arts, particularly the theatre and especially actresses. But he was wasting his life because he did not know what to do with it.

Plon-Plon had blotted his copybook several times. The military accused him of twice refusing a duel, and of failing to support the British at the battle of Inkerman in the Crimea.

Amongst his legion of mistresses had been the actress Rachel, the Comtesse de Lusignac, and Madame de Tourbey (whom he left for Cora). Marie-Anne de Tourbey had been a bottle-washer in Rheims (she eventually married Comte Victor Edgard de Loynes), while the great tragic actress Rachel had sung in the gutters as a child.

The birth of the Crown Prince to Napoléon III was a bitter blow to Plon-Plon, who had fancied his chances of succeeding to the throne. When he had to play his part in the child's grandiose christening in the Cathedral of Nôtre Dame, he was so choked with mortification that he could not announce the names of the baby he was holding miserably in his arms. His sister, Princess Mathilde, standing beside him as *Marraine* hissed: 'You can't get him to go back in! Get on with your duty Plon-Plon!'

Such was Prince Napoléon who considered himself a democrat and who, at the age of forty-three, took on Cora Pearl as his mistress. He gave her a key to his apartment in the Palais Royale and an allowance of 12,000 francs a month.

Cora had already experienced Plon-Plon's family life-style, when, in her new role of *maîtresse regnante*, she had spent a few nights at his request in his apartment at the Palais Royale. In the next room she could hear his wife, the uncomplaining Princess Clothilde, talking to their children. Cora dined in the same dining-room the Princess had just left, and was waited on by the same *maître d'hôtel*. '*Cela*,' Cora remembered (never shocked, but with her own standards of acceptable behaviour), '*m'a toujours gênée et impressionnée.*'

She obliged Plon-Plon from then on to visit her in her own home. He was soon deeply in love with her and madly jealous. Tough old cynic though he was, Plon-Plon wrote to her over the next ten years the painfully impassioned letters of a schoolboy.

Cora normally spent at least 25,000 francs a month, more than twice the sum Plon-Plon allowed her. She earned the difference in her customary way. Plon-Plon became suspicious and set spies on her. He involved her household staff, even getting round Cora's faithful companion-housekeeper, Eugénie Laforêt. He had gone too far. Cora refused to submit to his autocratic behaviour and his intrusion on her privacy.

'Frankly this did not suit me at all. What about my independence? My proud independence?' she recalled in her memoirs, 'I would keep my indepencence at all costs. After all, I could leave Plon-Plon whenever I wished.'

Plon-Plon, frightened of losing her, pleaded: 'I am not cruel. I want you to be contented and come to me in high spirits. But you must try to put your affairs in better order before they get worse . . .'

Next day the autocratic Plon-Plon called on her, abjectly, with the deed of a 200,000-franc mansion in the rue de Chaillot made out in her name. He also presented her with a second town house worth 425,000 francs in the rue des Bassins, to which he added, Cora noted meticulously, 200,000 francs as a lump sum.

Cora had tamed him. He was thereafter always kind and considerate to her, however badly he behaved to other people. Her gaiety and high spirits were necessary to him. She wrote in her memoirs: 'My first impression had been right. This man was an angel to those he liked – agreeable, witty and provocative in conversation. An angel, I repeat, to those who pleased him. Demon, rake, bad-tempered, insolent to everyone else. I ended by dominating him . . .'

It soon settled into a curiously cosy relationship. Plon-Plon kept his nightshirt and night-cap, lavishly embroidered with Napoléonic bees and eagles, at Cora's Chaillot home, and when he was not travelling somewhere or other, snatched every moment he could with her there. Plon-Plon was a compulsive traveller. Looking for something? Running away from something? He did not know himself. He had a circle of interesting friends, however, including Flaubert and Offenbach – so much better value for Cora than the mindless *jeunesse dorée* (indeed *jeunesse agée*) who frequented the top courtesans.

As with the Duc de Morny, Plon-Plon's exalted social and political status (for he had been Deputy for Corsica) brought Cora into the topmost circles, excepting only the Imperial receptions of the Tuileries, which she had no desire to attend anyway, and which bored Plon-Plon, who was obliged to attend, out of his mind.

Cora was now enjoying her life enormously – enjoying extravagant meticulously planned and perfectly organised entertaining in her lavish mansions in Paris and her sumptuous, cosy country château Beauséjour at Olivet. She especially delighted in her stable of splendid horses, cared for by her two excellent grooms who were imported from England and were the talk of Paris because they had never been observed to speak or smile in public. Cora, much as she enjoyed gambling in public, also liked playing her favourite game of Chinese Bézique in private. All was going merrily. Cora was keeping her golden place at the top without strain. But, like the Second Empire itself, Cora's gay life was spinning towards disaster.

Eight years had passed since Offenbach's operetta *Orphée aux Enfers* had enjoyed such a phenomenal success. Now it had been decided to revive it. Offenbach was busy preparing *La Grande-Duchesse de Gerolstein*, written for and planned to coincide with the opening of the Great Universal Paris Exhibition. Offenbach's colleague, Crémieux, was left in charge at the Bouffes.

The idea struck Crémieux that the role of Cupidon in *Orphée aux Enfers* might well be played by the dazzling Cora. The 'Queen of Uproar' as the Paris wits called her. He put it to her: Would she play Cupidon? a small, but showy part. And could she sing? But, of course, her speaking voice was so silvery she must have a good singing voice. Remembering her childhood home, dedicated to music practice, Cora laughed and accepted.

Plon-Plon was pleased and flattered. He was determined Cora must make a sensation in the part. He could not allow her, he protested, to use the Bouffes dressing room like a common actress (did she put the idea into his head?) – so he ordered Crémieux to buy the top floor of the house next door to the theatre and have a staircase specially constructed which would lead from her private dressing room there directly on to the stage of the Bouffes.

Cora set to work to make her rôle of Cupidon memorable. Gustave Doré designed a delicious costume: tiny tunic over tights, little blue wings and, on her red curls, a circlet of roses pierced by a diamond arrow. The tunic was cut very low. Ravishing buskins clasped her elegant ankles and shapely feet. The costume of course included a saucy bow and quiver of pretty arrows.

Cora's friend, Worth, made the costume, which, on Cora's instructions was liberally sprinkled with real diamonds. Her buskins not only sported large diamond buttons but (Cora's contribution to theatrical sensation) the soles were completely covered with real diamonds.

Meanwhile Crémieux, in his role of impressario, took Cora to Professor Colinvert to be coached in her tiny part. Cora thought it all a great joke. She recalled gaily: 'What zeal! What ardour! What diligent instructions, always tenderly repeated, always received with docility.' Cora noted complacently that both the professor and his wife, the famous singer, d'Urbine, had fallen madly in love with her:

Lessons in *l'amoroso*! *le crescendo*! *le rinforzando*! He pounded out my part, singing every word with me – miming every gesture with me – initiating me solemnly into all the professional tricks of putting a rôle across.

If Offenbach had been available he would certainly never have permitted this. He liked his singers' voices untrained. However, Cora knew the audience would be coming, not to hear her trill in the manner of operatic *divas*, but to see her capers and her costume – and it was all a lark anyway.

Cora did not appear on stage until the second tableau, with the Gods asleep on Mount Olympus, when she had to trip on and sing her small song:

Je suis Cupidon! Mon amour
A fait l'école buisonnière!
Je reviens au lever du jour
D'un petit voyage à Cythère
Un profond mystère
Câche mon retour!
Ils dorment tous!
Endormons nous!

Then in the fifth scene she had another two lines:

A Danae, ton adorée,
En pluie, un jour, tu te montras

In the final wild *Galope infernale* she joined in the revels.

At rehearsals Cora arrived very punctually in her magnificent carriage and swept on stage confidently. At the dress rehearsal two diamond buttons from her costume fell on to the stage; the dresser came to return them to Cora who told her to keep them. The director afterwards implored Cora to restrain herself; the dresser could not earn in two years what the diamond buttons were worth. If the theatre staff were given such lavish *pourboires* they would not report for work the next day, he explained. He was already having to pay them daily to ensure their attendance.

The opening night, Saturday, 26 January 1864, was sensational. The Bouffes was crammed with Cora's friends, lovers, artists, admirers, detractors, journalists and high society. Among them the Russian Princes Narishikine, Prince Achille (returned from Algeria), Prince Troubetskoi, the Duke of Hamilton, the Duke of Richelieu, the Duke of Brissac, Pasha Khalil Bey, the Duc de Rivoli, and the Prince de Sagan. The courtesans turned up in force: Adèle Courteois, Anna Deslions, Caroline Letessier, Giulia Barucci, Marguerite Bellanger, Marie Columbier and the rest. Tickets were changing hands at fantastic prices. Everyone wanted to see Cora. Plon-Plon was torn between pride and nervous anxiety.

The glittering audience waited breathlessly for Cora's first entrance. On she tripped to wild applause. For the first time in her life she was nervous. She began her song with her exaggerated bad French accent:

Je suis Kioupidon! Mon amour
a fait L'école byoussonière . . .

and got through it without mishap. The audience applauded and shouted '*bis*' so tempestuously that the orchestra struck up and Cora sang it again much better, with a saucy little dance kicking up her heels to show the audience her diamond soles. After this, all went well with her second solo:

à Danae ton adorée
En pluie un jour, tu te montras!

and, in the *Galope Infernale* her diamond soles flashed rainbows all over the Bouffes. Cora appears to have been obsessed by diamonds. They were, of course, a splendid proclamation of her success, and easily marketable in emergency. She had other more valuable jewels. But for Cora diamonds, and more diamonds, were what she wanted. Ludovic, Duc de Gramont–Caderousse, once quipped, 'If the *Frères Provençaux* served omelettes stuffed with diamonds, Cora would dine there every night!'

Cora's Cupidon was a *succès fou*. She was deluged with flowers and congratulations. All the newspapers gave rapturous notices. An Italian count offered 50,000 francs for her buskins (they were worth much more than that). Nestor Roquelplan of *Le Figaro* wrote a sonnet in her honour. Bookings were never better. And Crémieux was beside himself with joy.

This success maintained its momentum for twelve days. On the thirteenth evening an organised *claque* wrecked the performance. From all parts of the Bouffes, came rattling of large keys, and raucous voices yelling in unison: 'Go home British whore! We don't need you here! We have plenty of French Whores!'

Cora's defenders booed the booers, shouted back, stamped their feet and screamed. Pandemonium! Cora took no notice, calmly going on with her song. But it was no use. Finally she turned her back on the audience to make an extremely vulgar gesture to the *claque* and skipped off the stage.

The curtain was hastily rung down. Cora recorded in her memoirs:

Je jouai douze fois de suite. La Bande applaudit à tout casser. A la fin je fus sifflée. Je quittai les planches sans regret, comme sans desir d'y remonter. That's what glory is.

Who organised the *claque* which escaped in the pandemonium without being caught and identified? Certainly not hired nasties paid to do the job by jealous rivals. Something far more sinister, as Plon-Plon realized. It was a political demonstration.

The Emperor's attempts to stifle political criticism were not working. Revolutionaries, stirring up the impoverished workers of Belleville and Mélimontant, were secretly printing and distributing a smudgy revolutionary newspaper openly attacking the Emperor and his tinsel regime.

Young Georges Cavalier (so mis-shapen that his nickname was '*Pipe-en Bois*') was their leader, and it was he who led the *claque* that night. Their grudge was not particularly against Cora. It was against all foreign harlots making fortunes in Paris whilst the poor starved. It was against Imperial luxury and worsening conditions of the Paris poor.

The Emperor was totally immersed in his forthcoming Great Universal Exhibition which was going to bring the world to Paris to admire France's great industrial achievements and his Empire's military might.

If the common people had circuses, they would forget they lacked bread. That was his belief.

9
Leading to Sedan

Ten years is a long time when it includes a war, which was lost, a revolution, a siege, civil war and exile – and long, painful separation.

Why then did the unlikely Cora–Plon-Plon liaison last so long? These two unusual people obviously needed, and clearly complemented, each other. It was the Professor-Crouch's-favourite-daughter situation again – Cora, his chosen darling, comforting her brilliant but unlucky father–lover whose genius was not receiving the recognition it merited. Plon-Plon to the life. Cora was faithfully acting out her father's dreams for her – a brilliant hostess, the toast of the town, jewelled and gowned like an Empress – better than an Empress. Did Cora ever fear that Plon-Plon, like her father, might one day abandon her?

For Plon-Plon, Cora meant relaxation, in and out of bed, a lively young merry girl to cheer and soothe him. The hand fitted the glove exactly. He told her everything. She listened and sympathised, just as precocious little Emma had once listened and sympathised with her father.

Cora believed that her father was dead, even as she lay dying. But what did that matter? He was alive for her. He had possessed her heart, once and for all, when she was too young to defend herself. And perhaps in doing this he had unwittingly ensured Cora's success in her career, for she kept her emotions as carefully under control as she kept her meticulous accounts.

People have wondered for a century why so many men rushed to ruin themselves by Cora's extravagance. Did they hope to be immortalised by association with so glittering a star? Did they believe they would be missing something worth all their fortunes if they did not?

Such a one was the Irishman, James Whelpley, whose fortune of £80,000 Cora scampered through in two months. No doubt he explained to his grandchildren, whom he had deprived of their inheritance, that he might well have squandered his fortune gambling, whereas he had immortalised himself by his association with Cora Pearl. But when Cora wrote her memoirs she had completely forgotten him.

Cora prided herself on being business-like. To one client, who was slow to pay up, she wrote (keeping as she always did, a copy of her letter):

> It seems to me that since your wife's return you are neglecting me a little. While you owe certain duties to your family, there are also obligations to your connections and, because you accommodate the former, that is no reason to deprive the latter. So, my dear friend, hadn't you better show me some sign of life and the sooner the better? *à vous* . . .

Extravagant as Cora was, and she was well aware that her success depended on her extravagance, she nevertheless kept a sharp eye on the bills and would never permit herself to be cheated. She took her milliner, Madame de Florins, to court, complaining that she had been overcharged on a bill for 9,500 francs for various items including hats, trimmings, lace, a teagown, laced lined drawers and cambric under-wear. Madame de Florins lost the case and Cora had the satisfaction of having 1,000 francs knocked off her bill. She was getting mixed up with French law for the second time, but that she ignored.

Was Cora vain? She behaved with all the assurance of a beautiful woman which she knew she was not. She took good care of her splendid body, and loved all outdoor exercise: swimming, skating and especially horse-riding. The equestrian painting of her which hung in her mansion in the rue de Chaillot has disappeared. It was not a chocolate-cream Winterhalter but a fine painting of herself on horseback by François Emile de Lansac. Below it was a compliment in verse – probably composed by the Duc de Morny:

Et la riche Angleterre
Plus d'une fois dans l'eau jeta ses filets
Avant d'y retrouver une Perle aussi chère.

There was much fetishism at this period, of hands and feet. Especially hands. Cora, proud of her beautiful hands, had them cast in gold, silver and bronze, and also carved in marble. She gave these to her special friends and scattered them on her highly-polished occasional tables. Whatever happened to them all? Surely one or two must survive somewhere in some Paris junk-shop, whose proprietor has no idea of their origin.

The well-known sculptor, Gallois, carved Cora in marble, in twelve sittings. A lady begged to be allowed to be present.

She was, [Cora observed in her memoirs] charming, witty, gay. She returned several times to watch the sculptor at work, and me. 'Art,' she used to declare, 'is beautiful. But nature is much finer than art'.

Cora began to suspect the lady's motives when she developed this thesis further:

'What a pity the chisel cannot reproduce the slight movement of the breasts which are life itself.' Gallois smiled at this and I said to myself, 'He is sculpting me *et elle m'ausculte*,' and I took good care never to see the lady again.

Which gives the lie to those who have accused Cora of being a lesbian.

1867 was the year of the Great Universal Exhibition in Paris, which was to outdo the Prince Consort's famous Exhibition in Hyde Park. It was to be the culmination of Louis-Napoléon's ill-fated Second Empire, his swansong. All his schemes, all his plans, all his hopes for the future centred on this vast display of the marvels of French art and industry, French cuisine, French fashion, French Empire, the glories of glittering France.

All the other countries were invited to participate – Prussia, Russia, England, the USA, Africa and the rest. Every Emperor, King, President, Sultan, etc., was invited and they all accepted – to see, no doubt, that their own country's contribution was well displayed, and to enjoy an obligatory frolic in Paris.

Offenbach's new Operetta *La Grande-Duchesse de Gerolstein*, prudently set in the eighteenth century, satirised military pretensions, specifically Prussian military pretensions. The now famous singer, Hortense Schneider, was to play the leading part.

The Pavilion was divided into seven Regions, each representing a branch of human endeavour. 1867 was the year Lister introduced antisepsis, and Nobel invented dynamite.

The crowds who flocked to see the world's wonders were most fascinated, however, by the American rocking-chair. Britain backed up her display of heavy industrial machinery and loco-motives by a glimpse of the new wonder metal – aluminium – so rare and precious that Louis Napoléon immediately ordered for himself a complete aluminium dinner service.

Edifying, too, was the fine British display of missionary litera-ture: the Bible, tracts, hymns ancient and modern, translated into strange oriental, Asian and African languages and dialects for ignorant natives who could not read but whose souls had to be saved.

Herr Krupp's new fifty-ton steel gun, which it was claimed could fire a shell weighing as much as two small cannon, won a prize, though the French mocked it as a bad joke – for they still regarded Germans as a race of beer-swilling swaggerers without culture, and pedantic comic professors with the wrong kind of culture. The Prussian officers meanwhile displayed a flattering interest in the relief plans of all the great French fortresses.

The Emperor's own contribution to the Exhibition was the statue of an outsize marble nude, looking remarkably like Caroline Hassé, reclining on a large lion, entitled 'PEACE'.

There were also on show 'model workers' dwellings' (the Emperor's other special contribution, besides the statue of the fat-lady-on-the-lion). The workers from the slums of Belleville stared at them in silence: another pipe-dream of their hallucinating Emperor – who was awarded a prize, not for 'PEACE' but for those model workers' dwellings, none of which were ever to be realized.

Outside, the whores were making a packet from the stream of provincials and foreigners visiting Paris for the 'Expo'. Prosper Merimée observed:

These ladies are doing brilliant business and have raised their prices, like the butchers. Like them they too are selling fresh meat or what passes for it . . .

The grand climax to the Exhibition was the great Military Review at Longchamps, intended to impress the visiting Tzar but, above all, to overwhelm the King of Prussia and his gigantic Field Marshal,

Count von Bismarck, mountainous in his snow-white Cuirassier uniform, with an enormous brass spread-eagle topping his heavy helmet.

The Military Review should have mustered 60,000 troops but in the event it proved possible only to assemble 31,000. 'Their panache, however, took the breath away,' reported a witness.

To the boom of cannon from the fortress of Mont-Valérien the Emperor Louis-Napoléon arrived escorted by Spahis on splendid black chargers, with the Tzar on his right and King Wilhelm of Prussia on his left. There were grenadiers in high shakos, light infantry in yellow-striped tunics, *chasseurs* with green plumes, cavalry with long lances and fearsome helmets, turbaned Zouaves in red and blue, accompanied by saucy little *vivandières*, with kegs of brandy slung round their necks like St Bernard dogs. If the brass cannon looked somewhat undersized and antique, only the sharp-eyed Prussian officers noticed.

'*Vive l'Empereur*!' roared the crowds as each detachment swept past the Imperial stand.

The Review ended with a massed cavalry charge of ten thousand cuirassiers, carabiniers, scouts, lancers and hussars, halting in perfect unison less than five yards from the royal guests, and saluting with drawn sabres.

Nothing like it had ever been seen before. Soon, however, bad news began to accumulate. A shot was fired at the Tzar from a Pole in the crowd. It missed him but the white gloves of the Tzarevitch were stained with blood from the horse it wounded.

Worse still, the Emperor Maximilian I of Mexico was assassinated by Mexican nationalists at Quérétaro.

Manet painted a large picture of this historic event which he was not permitted to exhibit, lest it be thought to reflect on French Imperial policy.

The only royalty not present at the Review was the Emperor François-Joseph, in mourning for his murdered relation Maximilian (Emperor so briefly), and whose poor wife went mad afterwards.

A bad harvest was predicted, and from Algeria came depressing news of famine and cholera.

As for Offenbach's *Grande-Duchesse de Gerolstein*, which went much further than *Orphée aux Enfers*, this satire on military pretensions was a huge success.

Bismarck spent much time with Haenckel von Donnersmarck and Païva in Païva's grandiose Palace – planning and plotting. The Universal Exhibition gave him the perfect excuse to be in Paris just then, and to learn from them everything he wanted to know about the real state of the Emperor's fancy dress armies, and how loyal, or disloyal, his subjects were likely to be in the event of war.

The Great Universal Exhibition was a triumphant success. There was something for everybody. There were two entrances, one reserved for royalties, visiting royalties and resident royalties. Hortense Schneider, whose success as the 'Grande-Duchesse de Gerolstein' had gone to her head, drove up to the gate reserved for royalties, demanding admission as the 'Grande-Duchesse de Gerolstein', and was allowed in by the bewildered gate-keeper.

Cora, for once, was more discreet. Though she spent whole days there in Plon-Plon's private room, which he had furnished regardless of cost 'in the Turkish style', she declared in her memoirs: 'We went by separate routes.'

Plon–Plon had installed the new electric light in his Turkish room, amazing his guests by repeatedly switching it on and off. He spent much time drawing the new kinds of machinery on exhibit, and made a careful study of the new air-balloons in which Nadar (photographer and cartoonist, as well as daring balloonist) was giving demonstration flights over Paris.

The Grande-Duchesse Schneider was determined to wear the authentic blue sash of royalty with her stage costume. Censorship refused permission. She was so outraged she nearly walked out of the best and most remembered rôle in her career. However, she revenged herself by having a large portrait of herself painted in full Grande-Duchesse costume, including the forbidden sash.

What was reality? What was pretence? They were difficult to separate as the Second Empire rushed towards its doom.

Louis-Napoléon was now suffering from gall-stones. He was a sick man, bored and dispirited. Debauchery was taking its toll. He had lost what little grip he had left. At home immense riches, immense corruption, immense poverty. His Empress was increasingly obsessed by visions of 'gloire'.

During Louis-Napoléon's poverty-stricken Pretender years in London, when no hostess worth knowing cared to receive this apparently hopeless young hopeful, one lady had shown him great kindness. Countess Blessington, not in the topmost social circle because of her liaison with Count d'Orsay (whom everyone adored – wit, leader of fashion, sportsman, artist, handsome as a god and the soul of kindness), presided over an outstanding salon.

Here Louis-Napoléon met the most interesting people of talent in London, such as Charles Dickens and Disraeli. Lady Blessington took a lot of trouble to help this awkward young sprig of the defeated Napoléon I, who spoke French with a German accent and had no natural charm.

Much later, when he had become Emperor Louis-Napoléon and was enjoying the intoxicating fruits of success, Countess Blessington, travelling in France, met her former *protégé* at a reception.

The Emperor appeared not to know who she was. He asked coldly: '*Restez-vous longtemps à Paris, Madame?*'

Countess Blessington replied: '*Et vous, Sire?*' How right she was.

The glittering masked balls at the Tuileries, the elaborate parties at Compiègne, the showy ambassadorial receptions, underlined the one-dimensional quality of the Second Empire. It could not last. Soon the curtain must fall. But how soon?

The Emperor Louis–Napoléon came to the conclusion that France was ungovernable:

> When they have a Republic they want a King. When they have a King they want a Revolution. They always want something else. [He told Cobden] It is very difficult in France to make reforms. We make revolutions in France, not reforms.

The condition of the poor in France was deplorable. Bad bread and cheap wine was all they could afford. Agitators stirred up their grievances. Since the great Revolution how often had they risen, to be mown down, or promised reforms and a better life which never came? In London, Karl Marx, whose *Das Kapital* had just appeared, sat waiting for the Revolution he wrongly believed would break out in Germany.

In Paris there was very widespread prostitution and the feverish cult of 'pleasure'. All that mattered was money. The Stock Exchange ruled France.

The Emperor had set a bad example in loose living, but Parisians needed no encouragement. The Goncourt brothers quoted this prayer of the Second Empire:

Oh Lord! May my urine be less cloudy and my haemorrhoids less annoying. May I live long enough to make another 100,000 francs. May the Emperor stay in power so that my income will increase and may Anzin coal continue to rise on the Stock Market.

It was not a joke. It was perfectly serious. It was, in fact, an elderly male relative of the Goncourt brothers who prayed this prayer regularly every morning.

In honour of the Great Universal Exhibition, Cora joined forces with glamorous Giulia Barucci in giving an outstandingly sumptuous *Fête de Nuit* in the Bois de Boulogne. Six hunting horns saluted each newly-arrived guest. The orchestra played popular music from Offenbach's *Grande-Duchesse de Gerolstein*, alternating with Strauss waltzes. Bengal lights lit up the lake where pleasure boats glided. The food and wines, the guests agreed, were 'celestial'. And so on. A night to remember.

Thus Cora, as usual leading *la bande*, had the last word in the spectacular entertainment of the Second Empire. And Plon-Plon was proud of her success as that of a dazzling daughter.

10
Sedan

The Goncourts pinned down the unreality of the period in one sentence: 'It was like walking in a dream'.

Reality and fantasy became indistinguishable to Hortense Schneider, for one. She 'became' the Grande-Duchesse de Gerolstein, off stage as well as on stage, believing her hit song '*Ah! que j'aime les militaires!*' to the point of becoming infatuated with an utterly stupid young soldier only interested in duelling – soon dropping him for the real royalties who were flocking to her dressing-room to pay court and who were hardly more real.

The foreign royalties scrambling for seats were, however, concerned with more than *la* Schneider. They hoped to see their royal rivals satirised in Offenbach's smash-hit operetta, as much as they feared to see themselves satirised. The King of Prussia was there on the opening night, covertly watching his great Field Marshal Count von Bismarck to see how he was taking it. He was taking it very well for he had a better joke up his sleeve.

It is true that both the Tzar of Russia and his son Vladimir fell in love with *la* Schneider, as did Edward Prince of Wales, but it was her eight little dogs she liked best. They accompanied her in her *calèche* on her daily drive in the Bois de Boulogne and had their privileged seats in her theatre dressing-room. England was still popular with France, and so their names were Love, Pugg, Mimi, Wicky and so on. The French press, on the eve of the greatest catastrophe that ever befell France, was full of such tittle-tattle.

There were warning signs for those who knew where to look.

Great dressmakers (of whom Worth was outstanding) were seers – foretelling the future in the clothes they designed. Worth, helped by Cora who launched the new style the Empress stubbornly rejected, had come up with the 'bustle'.

The bustle was a political statement, though neither Worth nor Cora knew nor cared anything about politics. The smooth ample yardage of the crinoline dress, no longer buoyed out by the underlying crinoline cage, which Worth now discarded, was gathered up behind to fall in tempestuous confusion, like the slums of Belleville breaking from control.

The reign of the crinoline, like the reign of Louis-Napoléon, Eugénie and their rootless Second Empire, was on its way out. That was the message of Worth's bustle.

The Second Empire's days were numbered and it was going to end in hideous chaos. No-one knew it; no-one dared hint at it. But the grim future was beckoning. Like a dying insect, the Emperor still feebly waved his antennae – but to no purpose. Still the Imperial charade tottered on. The Empress Eugénie graciously sent the Queen of Tahiti (whose island was now French) the Imperial present of a large crinoline of crimson velvet, to instruct her in the niceties of civilisation. Then Polynesian Queen, accepting this tribute from one queen to another (though Eugénie was not massive enough to qualify by Polynesian standards as royalty), hung the red velvet crinoline above her from a tree like a canopy when receiving guests who warranted such an honour.

An invitation to visit Compiègne in November 1866 – one of eighty such invitations – greatly excited pretty Mrs Charles (Lillie) Moulton, American wife of a banker's son. A considerable wardrobe was necessary for the week's stay, as she wrote to a friend:

I was obliged to have about 20 dresses, 8 day costumes (counting my travelling suit) the green cloth dress for the hunt, which I was told was absolutely necessary, 7 ball dresses, 5 gowns for tea . . .

The Imperial train carried them from St Lazarre. Banquets, hunting, theatrical items and dancing, used up some of the long, dull days and longer evenings. The Empress had no conversation. The Emperor's moustaches wilted. Boredom settled on the guests, which the Emperor tried to relieve by playing dance music on a hurdy-gurdy.

The Universal Exhibition carried on jubilantly throughout the summer and autumn of 1867. At the end of October, workmen began dismantling it – a long line of Seine barges carrying off the debris, papier-mâché fragments of gaudy pavilions and once gay kiosks, including Plon-Plon's Turkish fantasy salon.

The Circus was officially over. Of course it had been a triumph – ten million visitors, plus no less than fifty-seven reigning royalties had visited the Great Exhibition. But what had all the expense and effort done for the common people, the workers of France who were still living in hunger and squalor? The glory was not for them.

A miner working in the Anzin Collieries (where the Company's dividends had tripled) was worse off during Louis-Napoléon's reign than before. His wages had increased by thirty per cent but the cost of living had increased by forty-five per cent. Haussmann's fine new boulevard had swept away some of the slums, to be sure, but had also driven the workers, who had been living there, out into the fringes of Paris where they now lived in appalling squalor. Even so, the rent of these dreadful hovels swallowed up one-third of their wages. Food took up another sixty per cent, though they ate very badly – horsemeat, introduced in 1862, was cheap but even then they could only afford very little of it.

Wages and working conditions in France were scandalous. Most working-class families in Paris had the family mattress in pledge at the pawnbroker's most of the time. Haussman declared in 1862 that: 'Over half the population in Paris lived in conditions of poverty bordering on destitution.' 17,000 working women in Paris earned between 50 centimes and 1 franc 25 centimes a day. The average wage for male workers was no more than 3 francs 81 centimes a day – and it was a long day of eleven hours beginning at 5 a.m.

Conditions were worse in France then in England, and even worse in Paris than in Mayhew's London. Moreover, the French worker was politically highly conscious of his miserable lot and the injustice he suffered. The Revolutions and uprisings of 1789, 1830 and 1848 had brought him no relief at all. The middle-class had grown rich, reaping the benefits, he believed, of his sacrifices and bloodshed. The readiness of French workers to rise against exploitation was strong. They thought in terms of barricades. Violence came readily to them. After all, what had they got to lose?

The students were no less affected. They could see no future for themselves either.

. . . Doctors without patients – lawyers without clients [Taine pointed out.] Dantons – Marats – Robespierres – St Justes in the bud.

Jules Vallés declared in his *Souvenirs d'un étudiant*:

The poorest students in Paris sometimes slept in graveyards – climbing surreptitiously over the walls, when the Police were not watching, to get in. With no future to look forward to they usually became drunks or insurgents.

The Emperor's hastily introduced 'democratic' reforms came too late. Nobody believed in them.

The Empress gave the last of her great masked fancy-dress balls at the Tuileries in 1869. Ominously, she appeared attired as Marie Antoinette. As the power of the Emperor visibly declined, and he was now suffering agonies from his large gall-stone, so the Empress Eugénie's power over him increased. She was one of those limited, stubborn women history throws up, to whom power means everything. Colette described her face as 'neutral, amiable and bored, like a moderately clever dog.' Her beauty was chocolate-cream, with cold eyes lit by unreason, and coiled auburn hair. She loved only power and delighted in war.

She was bitterly hated by her husband's relations – Plon-Plon (to whom the Emperor increasingly turned for advice now that the Duc de Morny had died) loathed her. And Princess Mathilde (the Emperor's cousin and erstwhile fiancée) held her in such bitter contempt as to be paranoiac. Apparently her American dentist admired her but no-one else did. She had not the gift of making herself popular, either with her relations or her subjects.

Plon-Plon could not make the Emperor understand the gravity of the situation, as blundering French diplomacy precipitated the unprepared Emperor into war against Prussia – a war in which the Empress insisted that he take 'supreme command'.

In vain did Plon-Plon warn him that an unsuccessful war would mean the end of the dynasty. The Empress was determined that the Emperor must wage it and win it.

There was a story circulating in France that at the time when France went to war against Austria, one of the Empress Eugénie's ladies-in-waiting sadly confessed to her that she always included a black outfit in her wardrobe – having several sons in the Army at the front, and one never knew . . . To console her the Empress declared:

Don't be foolish. The Army is the best possible place for our sons. War makes men of them. On the one hand they decimate the enemy – on the other they augment the population, for no young woman can resist our handsome sons in becoming military uniform.

On 15 July 1870, France declared war on Germany. She was without friends or allies.

Prussia was in a perfect state of military preparedness. Her officers had accurate relief maps for every part of France, and detailed plans of every French fortification, which was more than the French had. Well armed, well prepared, well drilled and furnished with all the information they needed, thanks to years of diligent spying by Count von Donnersmarck and Païva, the Prussian army was spoiling for a fight. Von Donnersmarck expected to be appointed President of Lorraine when Prussia had conquered France and seized Alsace and Lorraine, which she had long coveted.

The Empress Eugénie had taken care that Louis-Napoléon should be constantly reminded of his Imperial destiny. In a casket kept beside his bed, was a golden capsule ringed with jewels, in the centre of which, between two hollowed sapphires, was a fragment of the true Cross. This relic had been worn suspended on a chain, round the neck of Charlemagne. It had been given to Napoléon I by the clergy of Aix-la-Chapelle in 1804. It was said to assure the Empire to its possessor.

During that terribly dry 1870 summer of drought, crops failed in different parts of France. Horses had to be killed because there was no fodder for them. But this did not help the French workers because the price of horsemeat was too high for them.

The French Emperor now placed himself at the head of his unprepared army, in such pain from his gall-stone that he could hardly sit in his saddle. '*Louis!*' commanded the Empress, '*Fais ton devoir!*'

There was great excitement in France. At last *something* was happening to dispel the boredom which had followed the end of the Great Universal Exhibition. Mobs in the streets sang the *Marseillaise* (officially forbidden as too revolutionary), and shouted: '*Vive la guerre!*' The Zouaves had a parrot mascot they had taught to screech: '*à Berlin!*'

Figaro opened a subscription list to fund the presentation of a glass of brandy and a cigar to every French soldier in the campaign, and one patriotic publisher quickly brought out a Franco–German dictionary 'for the use of troops in Berlin.'

'Spies' were seen everywhere, and roughed up. Offenbach, despite his long residence in France and French citizenship, immediately fell out of favour and, since England declined to come to the aid of France, Gladstone was execrated and Cora, too, was out of favour.

Plon-Plon saw no outcome to this ill-advised war but disaster for France and ruin for himself. Cora, who did not try to understand what it was all about, did her best to cheer him up.

Not all the French were ecstatic at the thought of war. Flaubert wrote to George Sand:

> I am mortified with disgust at the stupidity of my countrymen . . . Their wild enthusiasm prompted by no intelligent motive, makes me long to live among the Bedouin.

The French High Command (consisting of aged and mediocre generals), counted on supplementing their obsolete weaponry with the renowned *chassepot*, and their latest 'secret' invention, the *mitrailleuse*, a precursor of the machine-gun, of which the French press had been boasting for months. It was to prove as unwieldy as a cannon but with much less range.

Marshal Leboeuf had long been boasting that the French Army was perfectly equipped and ready to the last gaiter-button. Nothing of the kind. Neither supplies nor troops were ready. Marshall Niel, the French Minister for War, who had asked for fifteen million francs, had been brushed off with five million. There were no proper reservists – the *Gardes Mobiles* (untrained, undisciplined and unwilling), were the substitute for reservists, and even they were little more than an idea, as France entered the war.

During the first few days of the war there was utter chaos. French troops in the north were sent to join their *dépôts* in the south, then to the east, then to the west. A retired major, observing the total confusion at the Gare de l'Est, commented reassuringly: 'Ah! It was just like that during the embarkment for the Crimea. The memory comforts me.'

Plon-Plon sent his wife, the Princess Clothilde, and their three children, to her relatives in Italy. The Paris mobs howled '*à Berlin*!' And the German mobs howled '*Nach Paris*!'

Though Offenbach was now hated, French soldiers marched to meet the foe to the music of his marches.

The Emperor had been warned of the folly of fighting Prussia. Baron Stoffel (French Military Attaché in Berlin) had for months been sending warnings that it would be fatal to fight the Prussians. Prévost Paradol, French Ambassador in Washington, had vainly implored the Emperor to think again: 'You will not go to Germany. You will be crushed in France. Believe me, I know the Prussians.' Then he had committed suicide.

In Prussia nothing whatever had been left to chance. Everything was ready and in perfect order. Within eighteen days of mobilisation Bismarck had produced a first-class army of 1,183,000 (nearly two million) troops; Von Moltke's perfectly organised Command, supplies, weapons and field hospitals, were ready for action. The new German railways had been precisely built to suit the requirements of this war. Prussian efficiency was terrifying.

But the French Army was in chaos. Generals could not find their brigades. Gunners had no idea where their guns were. When the troops finally arrived at their destination, exhausted and hungry, there were neither tents nor rations for them. There was no ammunition for their guns when they were finally located.

The French Navy was faring no better. The Admiral commanding at Brest was obliged to put to sea without vital charts of the Baltic and the North Sea.

The Emperor staked all on a rapid advance towards Germany. Here at last was action in which his troops could have a chance to excel. And they actually gained one victory at Saarbrücken, where the German advance forces were still weak.

Paris went mad with joy. Wild rumours spread through the city that General MacMahon had captured the German Crown Prince. A famous tenor was hoisted to the top of a Paris horse omnibus to sing the *Marseillaise* to the ecstatic mob below. Wishful thinking swept France. The Prussians were beaten. France was greater than ever . . . and in a surge of patriotic pride applauded the fourteen-year-old French Crown Prince (*bébé Empereur*) who now had had his baptism of fire and even picked up a German bullet from the battlefield for a souvenir.

But the rejoicing was short-lived. Within days the French Army, despite heroic and suicidal *sorties*, was completely beaten and in full retreat, which soon turned into a rout – the French generals issuing contradictory orders, the morale of the troops down to zero.

The *Gardes Mobiles*, decimated by great holes torn in their ranks by the deadly Prussian artillery (well out of range of their own *chassepots* and *mitrailleuses*), turned against their inept officers.

So began the disorderly retreat – but not to Paris. It was feared the broken army would demoralise the Parisians, who now had to get ready for the siege they had not anticipated. And in Paris there were already signs of uprising. Prosper Merimée wrote: 'We are heading towards a republic. And what a republic!'

On 16 August, the Emperor arrived at Châlons, in a third-class carriage, to find his army beaten and demoralised, soldiers lying about wounded, exhausted, out of control, their generals creeping about afraid to show themselves to their troops.

The eighteen battalions of *Gardes Mobiles*, whose officers were trying to rally them with the cry '*Vive l'Empereur!*' answered with shouts of '*Un – deux – trois – merde!*' as they stumbled off to the brothels and drinking dens of Châlons. Eventually, these *Gardes Mobiles* were winkled out and, unwisely, sent back to Paris.

The Emperor called a conference of his advisers for 17 August which Plon-Plon attended. The Emperor was listless. The only suggestion he offered was that Eugénie should be consulted. This suggestion was ignored. Plon-Plon pressed for the acceptance of General Trochu's proposals to defend Paris. Trochu was given the job of preparing Paris for a siege, on the understanding that the Emperor be kept out, lest his appearance provide a full-scale uprising.

There followed the tragedy of Sedan. Retreating, hundreds of starving French soldiers begged for food from French farmhouses where old crones spat on them and screamed at them, while the furious farmers barred their doors, threatening to fire on them.

The French Army became hopelessly trapped in Sedan with provisions for only a few days. The French cavalry in vain tried to extricate themselves by a series of recklessly gallant suicidal sorties. Inside the town the chaos was indescribable. Prussian shells burst from 400 cannon into the muddle of French troops and baggage trains, whilst soldiers, trying to fight their way out to continue fighting, were trampled to death.

The Emperor (his face rouged to hide the ravages of his illness), rode in despair outside the city walls, praying that a Prussian cannon ball would grant him release. But he had no luck. Finally, attended by his aide-de-camp Prince Achille Murat, he ordered the white flag to be hoisted over the Citadel. One of his generals immediately had it taken down again, crying: 'I will have no capitulation.' But the inevitable had to be faced. No-one would carry the white flag of truce to the Prussian High Command. But it had to be done. At last Prince Achille did the job, at 6.30 that evening, riding slowly through the Prussian lines under a flag of truce (earning himself a despised footnote in that part of their military history the French would like to forget), and handed the Prussian King a note from the French Emperor:

Since I could not die in the midst of my troops I can only put my sword in your Majesty's hands. I am your Majesty's good brother.

The world press was watching; General Sheridan, late of the American Civil War, the King of Prussia, his son the Prussian Crown Prince Moltka, Mr Russell of the London *Times* and, towering above them all, the giant implacable figure of Bismarck, determined to destroy France once and for all.

Bismarck was harsh. When Louis–Napoléon capitulated with 104,000 troops, he was sent to prison in Germany to be incarcerated in a *Schloss* that had once been the seat of his Uncle Jérome, King of Westphalia. The whole Prussian Army encamped at Sedan, sang Luther's *Old Hundred* in thanksgiving, and began to pack their equipment for the siege of Paris.

In Paris the wildest rumours circulated – anything was believed except the grim truth. Miraculous military victories – the King of Prussia gone mad – a rush to hang out flags and light lamps . . . then dispirited removal of the flags and lights.

On 3 September news of the capitulation at Sedan at last reached Paris. The Empress flew into a wild rage and retired to her boudoir to weep.

On 4 September, a serenely beautiful Sunday in Paris, crowds massed outside the Hôtel de Ville shouting: 'Abdication! Down with the Empire!'

The Senate continued arguing and debating. Futile. Parliament had taken to the streets.

De Concourt noted in his diary:

At the Café Brébant we sat down to dinner to the accompaniment of sad remarks on every side.

We spoke of the great defeat, of the impossibility of putting up an adequate defence – of the incompetence of the eleven men in the Government of National Defence . . .

Somebody remarked, 'Precision weapons are contrary to the French temperament. Shooting fast and charging with a bayonet – that's what our soldier needs to do. If he can't do that then he's paralysed . . .'

Somebody else pointed out:

We are surrounded by enormous stocks of petroleum which are stored at the Gates of Paris and are not allowed in because of the City toll . . . If the Prussians get hold of this petroleum . . . so it's all over. There's nothing left for us to do but rear a new generation to exact vengeance.

A few days later:

If the French nation had not been disintegrating, the Emperor's extraordinary mediocrity would not have robbed it of victory . . .

On 22 September:

On the heights of the Trocadéro there are groups of sightseers, including some immaculate Englishmen in *glacé*-kid gloves holding enormous field-glasses . . .

The Empress Eugénie fled, deserted by her servants who had shed their livery and pilfered as they left. The mob broke into the Tuileries, its main entrance now daubed with the slogan, PROPERTY OF THE PEOPLE. She did not know where to go nor whom to approach for help. Then she remembered her American dentist, Dr Evans, and it was he who smuggled her and her jewellery out of Paris and saw her off to England from Deauville, escorted by Sir John Burgoyne. She had left behind empty jewel-boxes and a half-eaten luncheon. The mob carefully erased all the Imperial symbols of bees and Ns and Imperial Eagles, and joyfully hurled busts of the deposed Emperor into the Seine.

An atmosphere of carnival prevailed. The weather was beautiful. The new regime (whatever kind it was going to be) seemed promising after months of shame and misery.

George Sand (then sixty-six years old) wrote:

This is the third awakening; it is beautiful beyond fancy . . . Hail to thee, Republic! Thou art in worthy hands, and a great people will march under thy banner after a bloody expiation.

Victor Hugo had returned to Paris to rouse the Republic. Cora Pearl was busy putting her beautiful Chaillot mansion in perfect order – for what? She had no idea.

11
Cora Finds a Job

'. . . Like walking in a dream.' But already the dream was turning into a nightmare.

The frolicking foreign royalties fled from Paris back to their own countries. The foreign millionaires bolted back to South America, North America, Turkey, Russia and Scandinavia. And with them fled most of the Paris courtesans, like hawks after their prey. Paris, which during the Second Empire had been the world's favourite luxury playground, now faced the horrors of a siege.

Many Parisians decided to bolt, and crowded the streets trying to get out with their household furniture and children. The slums could not have bolted, even had they so desired. But they did not so desire. Paris, they believed, was theirs and they would stay and starve and fight it out.

Cora, her two Paris mansions in immaculate order, waited. The English had become unpopular. But there were still many English people in Paris; long resident millionaire English noblemen, curious English tourists, resident English business people, as well as one enthusiastic young English art student, whose motto, she declared, was: 'Free love and Courbet!'

France had been declared a republic on 4 September. To Cora that meant nothing at all. What she had to worry about was her dependents: Salé, her faithful chef, Madame Laforêt, her rheumatic but devoted housekeeper, and most of all her beloved horses and their two English grooms. What was going to happen to them all?

And what was going to happen to all her possessions? Her two

84

beautiful mansions Plon-Plon had given her, her adored country house Beauséjour, her furniture, her bibelots, her jewels? But most important of all, what was going to happen to her horses?

Then Plon-Plon suddenly arrived, frantic, his carriage packed solid with valuable pictures and treasures. In panic he shouted, reverting to his customary foul speech which he had never used with Cora before: 'Cora! They are *** closing the Gates of Paris. There is no *** time to lose. We must *** get out at once. Bring your *** jewels. Leave *** everything else. We must *** seek refuge in London. Come at once!

Cora instantly made up her mind. Leave Paris? Leave everything she cared about? Leave her horses? Unthinkable!

'No, Plon-Plon! I'm staying put.'

'Cora,' he pleaded, 'Everything here will be destroyed. This is no place for you. You are English. This is not your war. I can look after you in England – Don't be a fool. Get your jewels. Come!'

Cora would not budge. It was not in her nature to run away. and what would become of her horses if she were not there to protect them? Those fearsome horsemeat shops . . .

Plon-Plon had no choice. 'Cora you are mad. I must go. I'll keep in touch with you somehow.' Off he went, his overloaded carriage creaking.

The Gates of Paris were indeed closing. Cora's first decision was to get her eight horses out of Paris to safety. She sent for her two English grooms and told them they were to take her horses to Cabourg, to a farm she knew where they and their grooms would be cared for. She gave them precise instructions and most of the money she had immediately available, besides some valuable jewellery they could sell if and when the cash ran out. She herself would accompany them to the Gates of Paris and get them through safely.

Reassured, and a little surprised, Madame Laforêt and Salé watched this new Cora; quite different from the gay and charming spendthrift they thought they knew. And France wasn't her country.

Madame Laforêt shed tears as she fastened Cora into her perfectly-fitting riding habit: 'It's all the fault of that Spanish demon Empress! . . . To think I share my name with such a monster!' She adjusted Cora's beautifully-cut riding skirt as carefully as though Cora were going for a gallop in the Bois. 'Be careful, Madame Cora,

I beg of you! . . . the streets are not safe! God protect you! God protect us all!'

When Cora, her eight splendid horses and her two po-faced English grooms arrived at the city gates they found tumult. Frantic families struggling to get out. Weeping children separated from their parents – cursing parents separated from their children – old grannies invoking Heaven's wrath against Bismarck, against the Prussians, against the ex-Empress Eugénie.

Into this bedlam Cora forced her way. Somehow she got them all safely through the gates and saw them off on their journey to Cabourg. She was thankful for the phlegmatic calm of her grooms, for she found parting from her horses the hardest part of the project. They were, she felt, not for the first time, so much nicer, cleaner, more beautiful, more intelligent than the squawking children all about her.

Now she had to get through the gates again back into Paris. The soldiers at the gates by now had lost all control of the panic-stricken mob. They were amazed, infuriated, to see Cora again.

'But you are *** mad!' they shouted. 'You've just managed to get out! Why the *** should you *** want to get in again? *** you! Be off!'

Cora gave them one of her looks which conveyed everything. She had a lover inside Paris – no doubt a soldier at the barricades . . . perhaps wounded? . . . They could understand, couldn't they? And whoever she was, hadn't they seen her clown's face before? She was clearly *somebody*. And what a figure!

'Oh, all right. Squeeze through then,' replied a soldier, 'and *bonne chance Madame!*'

Cora was not used to walking in the city streets. Her riding habit was impeding her. Everything round her was chaotic. Her *vélocipède* – that was going to come in useful. Meanwhile, she must get back home as fast as possible. She gathered up the train of her riding skirt over her arm and started briskly the long walk back to the rue de Chaillot.

Without Plon-Plon, Cora was her own mistress again, her destiny in her own hands. She felt absolute confidence in herself to make sense somehow out of the chaos into which Paris was disintegrating. The crowds in the streets were in ferment – braggart, fearful, vengeful – people were tearing up and trampling on vestiges of the ex-Emperor Louis-Napoléon's reign. At every street corner would-be politicians were shouting each other down. Cora watched a wild-haired student climb up a municipal building to tear the blue and white sections off the Tricolour flag, leaving only the red section fluttering. But her thoughts were elsewhere. She was thinking about her good friend Gustave Doré, who had been her lover and whom she had even thought of marrying.

Emotionally bound to his strong-willed mother, Doré longed for a life and a wife of his own. She understood Doré very well. For her own family background was that of talented struggling artists – of the patronised, not of the patrons. Cora's profession had taken her amongst privileged royalties and wealthy, idle socialites. She did not think much of them. Doré was different. He was a giver not a receiver. And truly talented.

But *marriage*? Never! Cora knew she could never extricate herself emotionally from her adored admiring father who had abandoned her. Just as Doré, she realized only too well, would never be able to make a life of his own apart from his emotionally ever-demanding mother.

No! No marriage, but instead 'my friend for ever'. Doré's charming cupidon costume he had designed for her to wear in *Orphée aux Enfers* was a tribute to his love for her. The diamond soles Cora had added to the buskins were her wry tribute to the values of the Second Empire.

Where Doré was now, she had no idea. But wherever he was he would certainly be drawing. Because he never stopped drawing. Perhaps he was with the disintegrating troops struggling in disorder back to Paris? Or struggling to get his mother and her belongings out of Paris as she had struggled to get her horses out?

In fact Doré, passionately French though born in Strasbourg, had joined the *Gardes Nationales*. Doré was emotionally committed to painting vast windy historic paintings which never succeeded. He knew, and Cora knew, that was because he could not achieve emotional independence from his devouring mother.

Cora understood the anguish of the brilliant men in her life whose achievements failed to reach their potential. Her father, 'Professor' Crouch, had prepared her for this understanding. Plon-Plon, so much cleverer than the Emperor, whose place he coveted; Morny, whose bastardy prevented his achieving more than brilliant string-pulling; Doré, so successful in his wood-engravings, so frustrated in his giant canvasses.

Children were running about the littered streets, waving little Tricolour flags, screaming '*Vive la République*!' – their ragged mothers massing outside the Hôtel-de-Ville howling obscenities against Bismarck and his hated Prussian armies. Everyone was shouting, yelling, cheering, cursing, denouncing. All this Cora observed without paying attention. She was clearing her orderly mind for something to come. She did not know what.

Now she saw wounded soldiers lying in the gutter, their uniforms torn and blood-stained. Some were already dead, crumpled like rag dolls; others bleeding into the gutter, where dirty litter lay uncleared, calling in pitiful voices on the Virgin Mary.

The crowds ignored them, kicked them aside, stepped over them, hissing 'Cowards!' – spat at them. Shameful reminders of the defeated French armies. No-one wanted to have anything to do with them.

It was a shock to Cora. She proceeded to do what surely any British woman would have done in the circumstances. She knelt down beside the nearest wounded soldier, tore her white linen stock in two and bandaged his bleeding head as well as she could. She questioned him and discovered that he was a Breton and spoke almost no French, which was a foreign language in Brittany. He had had almost no military training. He had no idea what the fighting was about. Nor had he any idea where or who the commander of his troop was. His best friend had been killed beside him outside Sedan. He turned his head aside and wept. He was not older than fifteen – one of the broken straggling remnants without hope, victim of mismanagement much higher up.

Cora looked at him. A Breton farmer's boy from some tiny farm, or maybe a fisherman's son from St. Briac. She was to learn later that death held no terrors for those devout peasant lads. What they most dreaded was the loss of a limb which would make them a useless burden to their hard-pressed families.

Cora had instantly made up her mind. She bundled up her riding jacket, propping the young soldier's sagging head on it. She told him, slowly and clearly, that help was coming, and ran the rest of her way home.

She announced to Madame Laforêt and Salé that she was going to turn her home into a military hospital (*ambulance* the French called it). Her bibelots must be stored away. Her luxurious carpets rolled up. Stores of food, fuel, linen checked. The wine-cellars checked . . . But first of all, Salé must go back and recover her wounded young soldier and bring him back. He would be their first patient. And she gave Salé a careful description of where he was to be found.

Cora sat down in her riding skirt and boots and crumpled shirt, and made out a list of what her *ambulance* was going to need: army hospital beds, litters, sheets, bandages, splints, medicines, invalid foods, trained nurses, doctors, a surgeon, a priest for the dying, transport . . .

Thank God for her *vélocipède*. She had kept it so long out of sentiment. Now it was going to be worth its weight in gold.

She read in Madame Laforêt's anxious face the unspoken question: 'What shall we use for money?' and reassured her. Not to worry. She had some money left. Still some valuable jewellery. When this was all gone a rich lover would be sure to turn up – even in the middle of a siege.

By the time Salé had staggered back carrying her wounded soldier on his back and Cora's riding jacket over his arm, a bowl of soup and a hot bath were waiting – besides towels and a clean shirt of Salé's (for Madame Laforêt refused to use Plon-Plon's bee-embroidered Imperial nightshirt, which she had carefully laundered and stored in lavender ready for his return some day).

Soon the wounded soldier, who believed he was dreaming, was bathed, fed and comfortably bedded down for the night in Cora's elegant boudoir. Cora, announcing that she was going to seek expert advice, peddled off to the Hospice of St Vincent and St Paul which was not far away. Cora was acquainted with the Mother Superior Beneventura, a large commanding lady with a Lorraine accent. Cora had seen her on several occasions in the early hours of the morning, outside the famous restaurants where Cora had been banqueting. The Mother Superior was always accompanied by two young nuns carrying large baskets. They were waiting for the restaurant's waiters to come out with the remains of the banquets – exquisite meats, delicate fish, rich desserts and fruits of the finest, thrown together into the kitchen pails which they tipped carelessly into the nun's baskets.

'*Pour les pauvres! Que le bon Dieu vous benisse!*' intoned the

Mother Superior, making the sign of the Cross over the baskets.

'*Voyez Madame*,' she whispered to Cora on one occasion, as Cora was being handed into her beautiful carriage by her coachman: 'It isn't safe on our Paris streets at this late hour, you understand, to let my nuns come unattended.'

The Mother Superior now greeted Cora briskly and listened to what she had to say. Yes, she could and would help. No use waiting for the army or the Government to move. Start straight away. She could provide a nursing sister, arrange for a visiting doctor-surgeon – of course the priest would come to attend dying soldiers – the local army depot could surely be bullied into providing hospital cots and litters and maybe even transport. She approved of the *vélocipède*. She wrote out a long list of medical necessities for Salé to take to the chemist and returned with Cora to inspect the accommodation for herself.

Madame Laforêt, who worshipped on Sundays at the Convent Chapel, made a deep curtsey to the Mother Superior, and Salé, a Provençale non-believer, made his best bow. The Mother Superior's verdict was that there was room for eight patients.

'Best take,' she said, 'only the badly wounded.' She inspected Cora's exquisite sheets – recognising the fine embroidery as the work of her nuns, abominably badly paid, she told Cora, and unfair to the starving embroiderers outside her convent who had to earn their living by their needle. The sheets must serve as shrouds, when necessary, and be torn into strips when bandages ran out.

Salé checked his stores of food and drink. There was plenty of *pâté de foie gras*, and the finest grey caviar. Nothing simple and easily digestible, however. The cellars were full of fine wines and the most expensive spirits. The Mother Superior who had served in an Algerian medical mission in her younger days, told Cora to be prepared for any emergency. She thumped Cora's handsome mahogany dining-table and declared it would serve for operations. She examined the windows and flung them all wide open. 'Fresh air,' she declared, 'is vital. Soldiers are dying like flies in all the big military French *ambulances* which keep their windows shut tight for fear of draughts.'

She and Cora got on splendidly – boldly cutting through red tape together. They respected each other's strong character, talent for organisation and endless capacity for dogged endurance. Their friendship was to last the rest of Cora's life.

Mother Beneventura advised Cora to put up a Red Cross flag. She had no faith that the Prussians would not fire on it, but she insisted it was right to try to protect the hospitals and offer the enemy a chance to behave like Christians.

Cora peddled off to see Monsieur Worth. His famous shop in the rue de la Paix was shuttered. He was upstairs with his family. Of course he was staying in Paris, he said. His wife was French. His two young sons half-French. His business was in Paris even if his clients had vanished (all except one or two wealthy American socialites, like Mrs Lilly Moulton, whom no wars could ever be allowed to interfere with their wardrobes, thank God).

Worth would not think of putting his workhands out of work – they could make uniforms if necessary. God knew the *Gardes Nationales* desperately needed proper uniforms instead of wearing anything they could lay hands on. And which flag should they choose? The Union Jack would be inappropriate, indeed tactless, with Gladstone so *non grata* at present. The Red Cross was the right flag. He showed Cora his own Red Cross flag, surely the most elegant in the world – exquisitely put together of white Lyons silk taffeta and crimson velvet. Then he looked at Cora sternly:

I know you, Madame Cora. You are capable in emergency of cutting up that beautiful scarlet bustle gown of Lyons silk we made you. Well, now you won't have to. Here are twenty metres of strong wide taffeta ribbon. Get Madame Laforêt to sew your red cross with it onto one of your strongest sheets.

Cora peddled back to the rue de Chaillot as fast as she could, and with all her household working on it, presently the Red Cross flag was unfurled above the roof of her *ambulance*.

There were soon eight military cots installed in Cora's salon; eight badly wounded soldiers (all Breton as it happened) being cared for – a nursing nun, a doctor visiting daily and a regular day and night service in action.

Cora, who did all the accounting, took her turn at night duty and soon helped in operations (for she proved to have steady nerves and the sight of blood did not upset her). She was a changed woman. She had left off make-up and wore her curly hair, undyed, beneath a plain linen cap. She dressed in a plain pre-war black dress (by

Worth), over which she tied one of Salé's large white aprons, and no jewellery at all. Her soft slippers moved silently over the spotless parquet. She, who had always been so wild and noisy, had learned to be quiet. And she felt fulfilled as never before.

Her patients adored her, never guessing that the flamboyant lady on horseback in the picture on the wall by Emile de Lanzac was the competent, quiet young woman who cared for them with such loving deftness.

In her memoirs Cora recalled her *ambulance* with pride and nostalgia:

Everything was done at my expense. The doctor had only his orders and his time to give. I paid for everything, including all the burial expenses. The dead were buried in my fine linen sheets. My patients were all well clothed and better fed than in other *ambulances*.

I loved them dearly, my little *moblots*. My hospital seemed to specialise in Bretons. Long afterwards many of them came to Paris to see me again. No other recognition has ever been sweeter to me. It was so free – so frank – the heart said all. We greeted each other like sharing good bread – real bread, not what we were obliged to eat during the war.

In the latter days of the Siege, *Pain Ferry* (named after the Minister who invented it) was issued on ration. It was composed of wheat, rice and straw and was described as tasting like 'old Panama hats picked out of gutters' – and also 'like sawdust, mud and potato skins'. This was the bread Cora referred to in her memoirs.

12
The Siege of Paris

The besieged French were convinced that Britain would now ally herself to France to repel the Prussians. Louis Blanc, the veteran Socialist who had spent so many years in exile in England, addressed a pamphlet to the British people:

Civilization is, for the moment, a prisoner in Paris!

Victor Hugo founted heroic epics:

Paris, which has been accustomed to amuse Mankind, will now terrify it. The World will be amazed . . .

Le Figaro announced:

In order that Paris, whose genius has given her the Empire of the World, should fall into the hands of the Barbarians there must cease to be a God in Heaven!

Such declarations embarrassed the British, who respond best in time of war to such exhortations as Bruce Bairnsfather's old Bill (in the First World War):

If you know of a better 'ole go to it!

or (in the Second World War) Winston Churchill's laconic:

Give us the tools, and we will finish the job.

When President Thiers was sent to London to plead for help, Mr Gladstone received him sympathetically but could offer nothing. Nor could the Tzar in St Petersburg. Nor could Cavour in Italy, though he did bring out the Comtesse di Castiglione from retirement to try her no-longer-youthful charms on Bismarck. All without success. Europe was frightened of Bismarck and his military Juggernaut.

Favre, the French Foreign Secretary, decided to appeal directly to Bismarck. The interview took place in the Château de Ferrières, whence the Baron de Rotheschild had been evicted. Bismarck was relentless and brutal. 'You are determined to destroy France!' cried Favre, bursting into tears. Queen Victoria telegraphed to King Wilhelm begging him 'to show magnanimity,' and was snubbed.

Bismarck's terms were so harsh that Favre dared not reveal them to the French nation. Paris was to be besieged and starved if she did not accept Bismarck's terms and, if that did not break her people, Paris was to be bombarded into submission.

Every nation has its genius as well as its weaknesses. The French, brilliant in gallant cavalry charges, could not govern themselves, whatever government they chose or had imposed on them. Now, with the Gates of Paris closed and the Prussians cutting off all communication with the outside world, the French inventive genius took over.

Nadar's balloons, which three years earlier had delighted the visitors to the Great Universal Exhibition, were trundled out. Patched and leaking, they were quickly mended and sent aloft over the heads of the astounded Prussians, carrying despatches, letters and politicians.

Clinging to the frail wicker basket, encouraged by shouts of '*Vive la France*!' Gambetta himself flew out first to rally the provinces. Soon there was a regular balloon mail. A factory was quickly set up to manufacture new balloons in the Gare d'Orléans, and when that was hit by Prussian shelling, the factory was moved to the Gare de l'Est. There was also the famous pigeon post which worked pretty well when the winds were neither too strong nor too contrary, and worked both ways, whereas the balloons could only work one way.

Plon-Plon, sunk in depression in London, somehow communicated with Cora. No doubt by pigeon post, possibly via the agony column in *The Times* which was available at the American Embassy in Paris till Bismarck stopped it.

Richard Wallace, natural son of the odious Marquis of Hertford, had now inherited his vast wealth and fabulous art collection.

Wallace, as generous as Hertford was mean, organised and financed two huge *ambulances*, one servicing fifty beds. He spent £100,000 to help the people of Paris during the Siege, including £8,000 for coal for the very poor during that terrible winter.

Particularly well organised was his BCF (British Charitable Fund). Of the 8,000 British people marooned in Paris during the Siege, about 800 were destitute. More fell into destitution, until the total reached 1,200. Each of these received a weekly ration of two ounces of Liebig's meat extract, one pound of rice, nine pounds of bread, and a little money. This ration kept them alive.

Cora's hospital set a pattern, which several of those few courtesans trapped in Paris followed. Blanche d'Antigny, whose mansion was much larger than Cora's, opened her *ambulance* for fifty wounded soldiers. Before long it became fashionable to nurse the wounded, and bored hostesses vied with one another to attract the most handsome *blessés*. One such lady, when offered two wounded Zouaves to nurse, asked for two blonds instead 'because she herself was brunette'.

Inside Paris the fearful sense of claustrophobic isolation was only lifted by the balloon flights. Parisians swore that their isolation was much worse than starvation and danger. They felt they might as well have been living on the moon. In the absence of news, the wildest wishful-thinking rumours circulated, such as:

29 September: The Prussians reported to be in full retreat.

6 October: A 'magic' tunnel has been secretly dug connecting Paris with the Provinces – so that, presently, sheep and cattle would be driven into the city to relieve hunger.

10 October: A revolution about to break out in Berlin.

20 October: A revolution about to erupt in England.

24 October: The Prussians have set fire to woods round Paris to suffocate Parisians.

One particular rumour was a *fact*: Païva (whose long-suffering Portuguese husband had at last persuaded the Pope to grant him a divorce), married Count Guido Henckel von Donnersmarck at the Lutheran Church in Paris on 28 October. She was then fifty-two, eleven years his senior. His wedding present to his bride was the magnificent three-strand diamond necklace of the ex-Empress Eugénie, which had come on to the market. Païva's revenge against the French Royal family was complete.

As for the Count, though the Siege had lasted only two months, he was so confident of Bismarck's victory and his own appointment as President of Lorraine (made before the fighting was even over), that he had felt it essential to transform the courtesan Viscondessa de Païva y Arajo, his mistress, into the Countess von Donnersmarck, his respectable wife. Then he sent her off to his castle in Silesia and joined the invading Prussian army.

Except for the rich who could afford to buy expensive food, hunger was now beginning to strike. Salt was desperately short. Children in Paris were beginning to die of scurvy.

By 12 November, the nets of the Seine fishermen were coming up empty. Not even a single gudgeon. By 13 November, milk had given out – gas had already given out. People had begun eating dogs, cats – even rats. Epidemics were starting. In one week in November, 500 people died of smallpox. Patriotism and courage (particularly in the slum districts of Paris) increased with hardship. Come what may, Bismarck must be resisted.

The *Marseillaise* thundered unceasingly from military bands. Floods of passionate oratory poured out. The patriotic mobs from the slums marched and demonstrated, believing (not without good cause) that the Thiers Government would sell France to Bismarck sooner than chance the Reds gaining control. What was lacking at all levels was common sense and organisation.

When Thiers finally urged the acceptance of Bismarck's harsh terms, the insurrection began. From the Hôtel de Ville, where 15,000 angry citizens were protesting, came shouts of 'No amnesty!' and '*Vive la Commune!*' And Bismarck, well informed of the situation inside Paris, refused to deal with Thiers, whose Government, he declared, 'No longer existed.'

Inside besieged Paris the National Guard organised itself, or more correctly, disorganised itself. Drilling and discipline hardly existed. Some regiments were made up of toughs from the slums of Belleville and Mélimontant; other regiments from the comfortable

Cora's father, 'Professor' William Nicholls Crouch, and (*below*) the popular ballad 'Kathleen Mavourneen' which he set to music in 1836.

An early engraving of Cora Pearl, 1864. (*BBC Hulton Picture Library.*)

Victor Masséna, third Duc de Rivoli, Cora's first link in her 'chain of gold'. (*M. de Lorenzo, coll. Musée Masséna, Nice.*)

Cora in a Worth ballgown. (*BBC Hulton Picture Library.*)

The Duc de Morny,
President of the
Jockey Club.

(Above right)
Gustave Doré, one of Cora's
favourite lovers.

Prince Napoléon, 'Plon-
Plon', and his wife Princess
Clothilde, daughter of
Victor Emmanuel II.

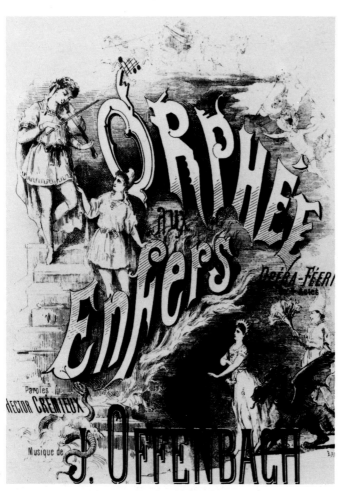

The music cover for
Offenbach's operetta *Orphée
aux Enfers*, in which Cora
(*below left*) played Cupidon in
its revival in 1867.

The original Cupidon
costume designed for the first
production in 1859.

Cora Pearl.

President Adolphe Thiers.

Home from the front.
Lithograph by Honoré Daumier.

A balloon factory was
established in the Gare
d'Orléans in order to
despatch letters and
politicians out of besieged
Paris, 1870.

'Queuing for rats' – a
drawing by Cham.

Louise Michel who set up a
women's battalion and was
later sentenced to life
imprisonment in the penal
colony of Nouméa.

The Vendôme Column,
demolished during the Paris
Commune of 1871. (*Stephen
Holder's collection.*)

Alexandre Duval.

8 Rue de Bassano. Cora spent
her remaining years
in the third-floor flat.

Cora's birth certificate
dated 1842.

CERTIFIED COPY GIVEN AT THE GENERAL REGISTER OFFICE, SOMERSET HOUSE, LONDON.

Superintendent Registrar's District of *East Stonehouse*.

1842. BIRTHS in the District of *East Stonehouse* in the County of *Devon*.

No.	When Born	Name, if any.	Sex.	Name and Surname of Father	Name and Maiden Surname of Mother	Rank or Profession of Father	Signature, Description, and Residence of Informant	When Registered	Signature of Registrar	Baptismal Name if added after Registration of Birth
163	Twenty third of February 1842 East Stonehouse	Emma Elizabeth	Girl	Frederick William Nicholls Cronch	Lydia Cronch formerly Pearson	Professor of Music	Lydia Cronch Mother Caroline Place East Stonehouse	Thirtieth of March 1842	J. Capron Registrar	

Certified to be a true Copy of an Entry in the Certified Copy of Entries in the Register Book of Births in the District of *East Stonehouse*. in the County of *Devon*. Given at the General Register Office, Somerset House, London, under the Seal of the Office, the *28th* day of *August* 186*0*.

By the Act of 6 & 7 William IV., c. 86, sect. 38, it is enacted, "That the Registrar General shall cause to be made a Seal of the said Register Office, and the Registrar General shall cause to be sealed or stamped therewith "all Certified Copies of Entries given in the said Office ; and all Certified Copies of Entries, purporting to be sealed or stamped with the Seal of the said Register Office, shall be received as evidence of the Birth, Death, or Marriage "to which the same relate, without any further or other proof of such Entry ; and no Certified Copy purporting to be given in the said Office shall be of any force or effect which is not sealed or stamped as aforesaid." The Act 24 & 25 Vict. c. 98, sect. 36, enacts that whosoever shall " unlawfully destroy, deface, or injure, or cause or permit to be destroyed, defaced, or injured, any Register of Births, Baptisms, Marriages, Deaths, or Burials "...or any Certified Copy of any such Register, or any part thereof ; or shall forge or fraudulently alter in any such Register any Entry relating to any Birth, Baptism, Marriage, Death, or Burial ...or any Certified Copy of such Register, or any part thereof ; ... or shall forge or counterfeit the Seal of or belonging to any Register Office ...or shall offer, utter, dispose of, or put off any such Register, Entry, Certified Copy, Certificate, or Seal, knowing the "same to be false, forged, or altered," shall be guilty of Felony, and shall be liable to be kept in Penal Servitude for Life or for any term not less than Three Years, or to be imprisoned for any term not exceeding Two Years, with or without hard labour, and with or without solitary confinement.

suburbs; one or two from the aristocratic arrondissements – amongst them the Baron de Rotheschild, eager to do his bit to defend Paris.

The wealthier units included a *vivandière*, the obligatory saucy girl in theatrical uniform, carrying a little keg of *eau-de-vie*. If the situation had not been so desperate it would have served for an Offenbach operetta.

There was a rampant black market, food hoarding and heavy speculation in food supplies. Worst hit were the wives of the poorest, obliged to queue for hours in the cold waiting for the shutters of the food stores to open, often unable to buy when they did open. The poor lived on bread and wine – vile bread, which gave their children enteritis – and the coarsest red wine which their husbands consumed in the bistros. Not a few of the poorest citizens of Paris sold their ration cards to richer citizens because they could not afford to buy even the miserable rations they were entitled to.

It was the first time in history that a city the size of Paris had been besieged, and, as the siege got under way, national disasters multiplied. So did lunatic inventions to frustrate the conquering Prussians.

As fantasy flourished, crazy inventions to defeat Bismarck poured into the offices of the Comité Scientifique in besieged Paris:

1. Poisoning the River Seine where it left Paris and flowed towards the Prussians.
2. 'Decomposing' the air surrounding the Prussian Army so that suffocation would bring the Siege to a halt.
3. Loosing all the ferocious animals from the Zoo to devour the Prussian army.
4. A musical *mitrailleuse* to lure the music-loving Prussian soldiers, by playing Wagner and Schubert, and then mow them down.
5. The '*doigt Prussique*' Borgia-inspired poison ring, whereby virtuous Paris ladies would repel the unwelcome advances of invading Prussian soldiers:

   The Prussian advances towards you. You put forth your hand. You prick him. He is dead and you are pure and tranquil.

Alix, the inventor of this *doigt Prussique*, surprisingly became a political representative of the 8th arrondissement and, not so surprisingly, ended up in a lunatic asylum.

On 29 November, the 'Great Sortie' (heroic and suicidal) was launched, when half-trained soldiers and untrained *Gardes Nationales* broke out of starving Paris in a vain attempt to drive away the Prussian besiegers. The inadequacies of the ambulance service caused terrible suffering in the bitter winter weather. This disaster did not prevent two further desperate and equally ill-fated sorties before the Siege ended.

Cora's small hospital continued to run smoothly and efficiently. It was a challenge, a job which she had undertaken and in which she was determined to succeed. Whereas her previous career had trained her only in extravagant luxury, Cora was now learning to waste nothing, to get the best out of the least, aware that her money was fast running out.

Only the celebrated American *Ambulance*, generously funded by friendly Americans, equalled Cora's in efficiency, the doctors agreed. And Cora had no resources other than her swiftly vanishing savings. There was heartbreak for Cora and her eight-bed *ambulance*, as well as the satisfaction of doing a vital job very well. It was agonising, after pulling through badly-wounded young soldiers and nursing them back to health, to release them into the army to die horribly in the hopeless sorties. The Mother Superior was outraged that Lister's discovery of antiseptics, which could have saved so many thousands of lives, had not been developed.

Cora's funds were almost used up now. She had to find money from somewhere for her *ambulance*. She owned another fine house in the rue des Bassins, but this was no moment to sell. Who wanted to buy an elegant mansion within range of Prussian cannon? Her beloved Beauséjour was heavily mortgaged. No, there was only one way for Cora to raise money. A rich lover was the answer.

Baron Abel Rogniat (from whom, it appears, Cora had bought her heavily mortgaged Château de Beauséjour) was his name. But where could they rendezvous in Paris, about to be under bombardment? Her Chaillot home was now the hospital for which Cora needed money – Beauséjour was inaccessible. I believe her liaison with Baron Rogniat took place at her other mansion in the rue des Bassins.

Perhaps it had been let? But there is seldom a problem without any solution. And certainly discreet Madame Laforêt would have made all the arrangements. Probably Cora used her indispensable *vélocipède* to travel between her hospital in the rue de Chaillot and her mansion in the rue des Bassins.

It was not until his fortune had been entirely swallowed up by Cora's *ambulance* that the Baron bowed out, retiring to Cevita Vecchita in his native Italy to start a soap factory and, hopefully, make another fortune.

'Famine is on the horizon,' reported Goncourt. Fresh vegetables were unobtainable and horsemeat an expensive delicacy. Parisians had begun to kill and eat their pets. Wary cats were shrinking from a caress which they sensed was assessing their meat potential. Rat-hunting had become a patriotic duty. Domestic rats were selling at a higher price than sewer rats. The renowned chef of the Jockey Club invented rich sauces to accompany his *Salmi de Rats* and Rat Pie.

Portions of wolves appeared for sale at a fashionable butchers on the Faubourg St Honoré. Kangaroo was served at the Goncourts' favourite restaurant *Chez Brabant*, and camel was being snapped up at the fashionable butcher, Roos. The only reason the hippo-potamus at the Zoo survived was because no butcher could afford to pay the 80,000 francs demanded.

Prices soared out of control. There was unchecked speculation in anything edible. The poor continued to exist on rationed bread, now so bad that it caused grave illnesses in adults as well as children. The cheap raw wine consumed in the bistros, however, never ran out, and on this the *Gardes Nationale's* pay of 1½ francs per day was spent.

At the Château de Ferrières Bismarck and his colleagues, disturbed by the bad effect their delay in achieving complete victory was having inside Germany, decided to bombard Paris.

On 5 January, the first shells burst over the left bank, killing a little girl on her way home from school, blowing an old woman's head off, and killing six women in a food queue.

Then, between 300 and 400 Prussian shells were fired into Paris every day. Despite their large Red Cross flags, Paris hospitals became targets. Cora's own hospital in the rue de Chaillot did not escape damage.

Cora, who had always believed Païva (now the Countess von Donnersmarck) to be a spy, observed that, though the other mansions on the Champs Elysées were being damaged by Prussian shelling, Païva's Hollywood extravaganza was untouched.

That winter the hunger and terrible cold were harder to bear than the bombing. Anything that would burn was taken from the gardens of the fashionable districts. Trees on the *grands boulevards* were cut down and carried off for firewood. The Rotheschilds paid for garments for 40,000 children and 40,000 adults freezing to death, their own clothes having been pawned. Newspaper shirts were recommended as epidemics of typhoid and smallpox added to the toll from lung diseases sweeping through Paris.

By 15 January only fear of a 'Red Rebellion' prevented the Thiers Government from surrendering to Bismarck. There was only enough food left for a few days' scanty rations. The Red districts demanded 'No Surrender' and that the Commune should replace the Thiers Government.

The weather, that winter in Paris, was the coldest ever recorded.

A last desperate sortie was launched (more to keep the undisciplined *Gardes Nationales* from storming the Hôtel de Ville, than in hope of damaging the Prussians). It was defeated with terrible loss of life – the losses amongst the *Gardes Nationales* were worst of all. They had been 'bled' by design. The survivors, stumbling back into Paris, broken and bleeding, had every right to cry in protest: '*Nous sommes trahis!*'

Belleville, enraged by the slaughter of the untrained National Guards, marched with drums beating to seize food and arms from municipal stores and on to the Hôtel de Ville.

Presently, in the chaos, Frenchmen were firing on Frenchmen.

'Civil war is but a few yards away – famine a few hours,' wrote Jules Favre, deciding on an immediate armistice with Bismarck on any terms. Bismarck had been urging him for weeks to provoke an uprising in order not to have to quell a bigger one. The Government, if it could still be so called, broke up.

In the last few days of the Siege, Archibald Forbes (correspondent of the *Daily News*) reported:

One small shrivelled cabbage cost 2 francs
One small leek cost 1 franc
A cat (emaciated) cost 45 francs.

For those who care for figures: The Siege had cost 28,450 casualties (military and National Guards), 6,251 civilian lives, and 4,800 children's lives.

13
The Commune

During the reign of Louis-Philippe, his policy of comfortable middle-class inertia so bored his subjects that they welcomed the excitement of the coup which set Louis-Napoléon on the throne.

What Paris feared most, then as now, was *ennui* – boredom. Any danger, any conflict, was preferable to *ennui*. And perhaps the worst horror of the starvation Siege was the long *ennui* of the Parisians entombed in their besieged city – isolated, cut off, forced in on themselves without distraction. Their days were, Goncourt wrote: 'VERY EMPTY – VERY EMPTY – VERY EMPTY.' That explains the lack of panic when the German bombardment of Paris began; it was distracting, almost welcome.

There had been only one exciting event in Louis-Philippe's reign, when the American painter, George Catlin, brought a group of wild American–Indian natives to Paris in 1845, to dance their war dances at the Salle Valentino. Victor Hugo, Baudelaire and George Sand went again and again. George Sand could not contain her thrill of terror. She wrote:

. . . A kind of delirious rage seemed to transport them – raucous cries, barks, roars, shrill whistles and the war-cry which the Indian makes by putting his fingers on his lips and which, uttered far off in the deserts, freezes the strayed traveller with fear . . . A cold sweat came over me. I believed I was witnessing the real scalping of some vanquished enemy or some still more horrible torture . . .

Catlin toured his natives in Belgium afterwards, where eight of them contracted smallpox and two died. The tour was abandoned. And

George Sand returned to her romantic idealism about the working-class and the radiant era which would dawn once the workers took power (for at that time she had a lover who was a left-wing leader).

Revolutions, however, are not made by benevolent idealists. They are made by starving, embittered outcasts, revenging themselves on those who have reduced them to their desperate condition. And revolutions are led or, as history reveals, usually misled, by scheming politicians, distrustful of one another and avid for power.

Bismarck had now set up his headquarters in Versailles, where the German King had been crowned Emperor of all Germany – united at last: 'Already one race, one people, we are now one nation.' Hitler was to echo these words seventy years later.

The bitter cold continued all that terrible winter. Even the well-fed German soldiers suffered from the icy weather. The delayed victory was now affecting the German troops as well as the Germans at home. A cable from the Governor of Berlin to Bismarck expressed fears of insurrection.

This was what Karl Marx, watching every move from London, had been counting on. He considered only the well-organised German proletariat were capable of carrying out a successful revolution. He had no faith in the Paris insurgents at all – he considered them 'unorganised and unorganisable rabble', and was taken by surprise when their Commune was declared.

When peace preliminaries were discussed, Haenckel von Donnersmarck and Bleichroeder (the German Minister of Finance), on behalf of Bismarck, went over the financial clauses of the Treaty with Thiers. Bleichroeder suggested that France should pay war indemnities of three thousand million francs. Haenckel von Donnersmarck made the German Chancellor demand six thousand million francs.

But von Donnersmarck's scheme to please Bismarck by totally crushing France proved unworkable. Thiers had just decreed that all rents in Paris unpaid during the Siege were now to be paid in full, along with other harsh measures impossible for the ruined Parisians to obey. Strong British representation persuaded Bleichroeder to think again. Finally, the indemnity was fixed at five thousand million francs. 'So ponderous, so crushing, so mortal for France,' mourned Goncourt.

Rather than fight a losing war on two fronts, Foreign Minister Favre arranged for a ceasefire on 23 January. Bismarck was at his most brutal. The dictator, corsetted in his tight white Cuirassier uniform, had everything his own way.

Said Favre: 'God only knows what the Paris populace will do to us when we are compelled to tell them the truth.'

France would not only have to pay a war indemnity of five thousand million francs, but also surrender perimeter forts, throwing their rampart guns into the moats, and the French army would have to surrender its arms and Colours. But *officers were to be allowed to keep their swords.* (Favre fought hard for this one concession.)

The Armistice was to last until 19 February – giving time to revictual starving Paris and elect an assembly which would discuss whether or not to continue the war, and on what terms to conclude a definite peace treaty.

Finally, Favre begged even harder for a last favour: that Paris be allowed to fire the final shot of the Siege. This Bismarck contemptuously granted.

To Cora, struggling desperately to keep her hospital solvent, it all seemed a cruel farce. Her heart went out to the Mother Superior praying for her beloved Lorraine which Metternich was seizing. But the French officers kept their swords and the final shot of the Siege was duly fired by a French cannon.

Paris was outraged by the Armistice. Edward Child, a young English jewellery salesman resident in Paris, who had joined the National Guard to help defend Paris, resigned in disgust. '400,000 men capitulating!' he wrote in his diary, '. . . granted half of them no use as soldiers, *soit* 200,000. I pity the people but scorn the chiefs . . .'

There was still a vast store of unused arms in Paris, especially in Montmartre where the cannon, bought by the workers with their own money, stood unused. 130 days of siege, to end like this!

But for the working population of Paris, who had borne the brunt of the Siege and suffered the worst hunger and shelling, the war hadn't ended. They, whose lives were crushed at the very bottom of the social pyramid, remained totally loyal to the country which had given them nothing but misery.

They cherished it because it *was* their country – all they had, or were going to have. For they were determined to make it theirs by driving out the Prussian invaders along with the Thiers Government. The Commune was their answer to Bismarck and Thiers.

And here we must make it clear what 'Commune' and 'Communist' then meant. It was the Paris Town Council directing the civil life of Paris – like the GLC looking after London's health, transport, parks, education, etc. The Paris working-class had endured a wretched life. Now they were determined to seize Municipal power to better their conditions.

Cora understood nothing of all this. Eugénie Laforêt and Salé argued politics endlessly. Cora was preoccupied with her hospital.

With the Armistice, at last food began to flow into starving Paris. The Kaiser ordered six million army rations to be sent in (not from pity, it seems, but anxiety). Gladstone's Government sprang into action. Navy ships were requisitioned, quickly loaded with army food supplies of every kind, and sent across the Channel. At Deptford twenty-four great ovens worked day and night baking bread and hard tack. The Lord Mayor's Relief Fund was inundated with donations.

The London Relief Committee sent 10,000 tons of flour, 450 tons of rice, 900 tons of biscuits, 360 tons of fish, 4,000 tons of fuel and 7,000 head of livestock. America sent two million dollars worth of food.

But conditions in France were in such anarchy that distribution did not go smoothly. At Le Havre no-one could be found even to unload the relief ships. The railways were not functioning. Minor hitches caused offence, as when the French authorities insisted on sending back pheasants (donated by some British landowners), explaining rather smugly:

. . . these things are for the aristocracy and not for the people: it would be more prudent not to distribute them.

(Unlike Vaillant-Couturier, the Communist leader in France sixty years later, who was all for 'Champagne for the Workers'.)

In Paris, drums heralded the arrival of the first food convoy on 4 February. By the 7th the trickle of food became a torrent, headed by a long train of wagons containing food from Britain.

Britain became popular again in French eyes. Cora was back in favour – though in her hospital (as in her household) and, of course, with the *poilus* and the *mobiles* in the army, she had never been other than adored. It is to be hoped that she managed to acquire some donated food for her patients – for distribution was riotous and wasteful.

The police could not control the crowds. There was fighting and pillage at Les Halles, and eggs, vegetables and butter trampled underfoot in the rioting. There was also serious inequality in the distribution of food – the poor remaining often hungry. Scurvy was beginning to increase again. Those well-meant pheasants would have been welcome had they been allowed to be distributed in the slums. Altogether Paris, though rescued from starvation, was in a state of frenzy with disappointment, humiliation and apprehension of the future.

Trochu (when Governor of Paris) had declared: 'The Governor of Paris will not capitulate.' And had capitulated.

Favre (Foreign Secretary) had vowed: 'Not an inch of our territory, nor a stone of our fortresses.' And had signed away Alsace-Lorraine and agreed to the dismantling of the fortresses.

President Thiers, who had sworn: 'The enemy shall not enter Paris,' now agreed to Bismarck's demand for a Victory march and two-day occupation of Paris.

The National Guards (untrained, excitable but loyal to Paris and its defenders) seized arms and ammunition and carried them off into the slum districts of Belleville, Mélimontant, Villejuif and especially Montmartre, ready to resist attack from Bismarck's troops or from 'traitor' Thiers' soldiers.

On 1 March, in glorious spring weather, 30,000 Prussian and German troops with bands playing, flags flying and splendid horses showing their paces, made their way (though some Uhlans lost their bearings in the debris and had to ask French onlookers to direct them) through the desolate Bois de Boulogne, now unkempt and denuded of its fine trees. In splendid order they goosestepped through the Champs-Elysées, where Count Haenckel von Donnersmarck (prematurely President of Lorraine), in full military glory, stood on the balcony of his undamaged Hollywood-style Palace, greeting each regiment as it passed.

The costly architectural whimsies all around had not escaped Bismarck's shelling. Plon-Plon's Palais Pompéien (which he had prudently sold in 1866 for £70,000); Émile de Giradin's Roman

Palace; the Marquis of Quinsone's Gothic Castle; Jules de Lessep's Tunisian Château; the Duke of Brunswick's Pink Hotel; the late Duc de Morny's fetching Museum; all were battered and derelict. Only von Donnersmarck's neo-renaissance Païva Palace was intact. Cora and the Mother Superior stayed indoors with the shutters closed, the Red Cross flag floating above their shell-damaged hospital, where the last of their *mobiles* were either convalescent or soon to die.

But the pavements in this luxurious section of Paris were crowded with middle-class Parisians anxious not to miss a fine show. It was not only the foreign correspondents who admired the parade, but also the French onlookers who could not conceal their homage to their conquerors.

I well remember talking to Paris friends – after the Second World War – who had witnessed the Nazi Victory Parade through Paris.

When we saw those tall, handpicked, perfectly drilled, blond young Nazi soldiers, looking down on us like Gods from their great war-machines, we thought: 'They are better soldiers than we are. We deserve to be conquered by them!'

This is the reverse side of the theatrical bravado with which Louis-Napoléon had corrupted France. Once footlights were switched off, what was there left but starving mummers stranded on their broken-down stage?

The English journalists, dazzled by Bismarck's victory parade, let themselves go:

Out rings the clarion of the trumpets! Clash goes the music of the kettledrums, tempered by the sweet notes of the ophicleide! . . .

wrote Archibald Forbes for the *Daily News*.

The spectacle was one of the most thrilling I ever witnessed

declared another military correspondent. It was better than an opera.

After the parade ended the German troops were allowed to amuse themselves visiting the Tuileries Gardens, crowning themselves with laurels and jackbooting about Paris, except in the districts of Belleville, Montmartre and Mélimontant which were *verboten* by their officers, who were taking no chances.

As soon as the victory marchers withdrew, with banners flying, bands thundering and a final blood-curdling (or heart-warming – it depends which side you are on) cheer, the French scrubbed all the streets where German soldiers had set foot with Condy's fluid, and purified the sacred air of Paris by lighting great disinfecting bonfires.

The French have never got over it. I was in Paris when the news broke of French defeat at Bien Den Phui in Vietnam in 1954. All entertainments were cancelled. On the Underground a grizzled veteran French soldier sitting opposite me burst into tears, tore his medals from his uniform and cast them out of the window, sobbing: *'Nous sommes foutus!'*

Whilst the streets of Paris were being disinfected and purified on 3 March, anyone suspected of having been friendly to the German troops was manhandled. Archibald Forbes (who had politely doffed his hat to the German Crown Prince, whom he knew), was beaten up and narrowly escaped being thrown into the Seine. As for any woman even suspected of civility to the invading soldiers, she had her clothes torn off, was tarred and feathered and had her hair torn out or shaved off; another grim ritual which was repeated in the First and Second World Wars.

Thiers was alarmed to find the National Guard were definitely not on his side. On the march to Versailles, where he had set up his Government, they did not obey their officers, refusing to salute them and declaring openly they would not fight against their brethren in Paris. Thiers sent back some of his regular troops to resume occupation of the Hôtel de Ville. He now appointed Admiral Saisset to command the National Guard and sent him back into Paris to see what loyal National Guards he could rally.

Since this book is about women in a man's world, we must not omit two women who played their parts in the Commune.

Both were bastards whose fathers had abandoned them. Louise Michel, daughter (on the wrong side of the blanket) of a French landowner and his housemaid, was forty at the time of the Commune, when she became known as 'the red virgin'. She had been a school teacher. She was plain, thin, heroic and romantic, absolutely fearless and a deadly shot. Always where the fighting was fiercest, with her rifle and her keg of *eau-de-vie*, it seemed miraculous that she was never even wounded. She dreamed of a heroic death on the barricades. During a lull in the fighting she was seen on one occasion to enter an abandoned church and play classical music on the organ.

She had come to the conclusion that the only way to deal with 'public enemy Thiers' was through assassination. When the Committee rejected her plea to be given this task, she disguised herself and made the journey to Versailles (where she could easily have done the job without sanction) and returned to Paris to report on its feasibility and demonstrate her obedience to orders. Besides setting up a women's battalion, she loved and took care of her old mother.

Aiding Louise Michel was Elizavetta Dimitrieva, a beautiful young Russian woman of many love affairs. Bastard daughter of a Tzarist cavalry officer, she had been well educated in St Petersburg, where she joined a group of political dissidents. In Switzerland she met the international group of political plotters. In London she became a close friend of Karl Marx's daughters. Marx sent her to Paris to help Louise Michel organise women's groups in the Commune and report back to him exactly what was going on. She was wounded when Thiers' troops invaded Paris.

The demonstration of 15,000 outside the Hôtel de Ville, which triggered off the Commune, began peacefully. It included many women and children as well as two and a half thousand National Guards, disorganised as usual, but united in denouncing violence. All the demonstrators were opposed to violence, of which they had suffered more than a bellyful and, they declared, had brought them nothing but shame and disaster.

Suddenly a shot was fired into the crowd from the Hôtel de Ville. Then came a fusillade of firing from every window of the Hôtel de Ville into the now panicking demonstration. Louise Michel, firing to kill from behind an overturned bus, rallied the demonstrators. The French were firing on the French. Thiers had declared war on Paris. The dead, mostly women and children, were dragged away to be buried in the already overcrowded cemeteries.

Pretty young American socialite, Mrs Lillie Moulton, who had been away from Paris during the Siege, chose this moment to visit her couturier, Worth, to order her spring wardrobe. She witnessed what became known as the 'rue de la Paix massacre'.

A group of retired colonels, little shopkeepers, vegetarians, etc. who called themselves Friends of Order were marching in a small demonstration towards the Hôtel de Ville. (Why not? Everybody else did). They were unarmed, except for the odd ornamental sword-stick, a hidden pistol or two on the persons of the more nervous and, of course, walking-sticks for the elderly. Their banners were inscribed 'Pour la Paix'. Their genteel slogans were 'Vive l'Assemblée' and 'Vive la République'.

As they turned into the rue de la Paix, they collided, head-on, with a detachment of trigger-happy National Guards. Insults were exchanged. Who fired first? No-one ever knew. But Lillie Moulton (who had picked her way through the streets and obligingly added a cobble to the various barricades being set up, which all passers-by were invited to do in the name of friendship), had a grandstand view of what happened next. From an upstairs window of Worth's fine establishment:

Looking down, the street was filled with smoke – screams and terrified groans reached our ears ... The street was filled with the dead and wounded. The living members of the *Amis* scampered off as fast as their legs would carry them while the wounded were left to the care of the shopkeepers ... the dead were abandoned where they fell ...

As the front ranks of the National Guard pushed forward, they were fired on by their own rear ranks. It was a muddle of misunderstanding and horror; more common in conflicts than war historians care to mention.

Mrs Moulton was escorted back home and put to bed with a cup of soothing Camomile tea before returning to Versailles.

The rift between Paris and Versailles was now beyond repair. Admiral Saisset left Paris in disguise to report his findings to Thiers in Versailles – declaring he would need a force of at least 300,000 trained troops to crush the insurgents in Paris. 'I have not got four men and a child to give you,' Thiers replied in his squeaky voice. Nightly he orated against the use of force (reported Lillie Moulton), cheered by the ladies who waved their lace handkerchiefs every time he mentioned 'the destiny of France'.

Thiers set himself to recruit an army of professional soldiers, armed with cannon and every weapon he could lay hands on, to invade Paris and destroy the Commune they were now setting up.

The later crazed excesses of harpies and ruffians from the slums of Paris, should not blind us to the admirably sensible aims with which the Commune launched itself. It was, moreover, (like the Government Franco overthrew in Spain sixty years later) legally elected by the citizens of Paris with a four to one majority.

The inauguration of the Commune was splendid. 20,000 National Guards marched (for once in perfect formation), many carrying loaves impaled on their bayonets as symbols of their objectives: Peace, food, progress. Each battalion was of course preceded by an attractive young woman *cantinière* in a kepi and bloomers, with a cask of *eau-de-vie* suspended over her shoulder.

Edward Child, who had quit Paris for England because he couldn't stand it, had now returned to Paris because he couldn't live without it.

The need for reform was only too obvious. Louis Rossel, a professional middle-class French officer declared:

These people have good reason for fighting. They fight that their children may be less puny, less scrofulous, and less full of failings than themselves.

As to the glories of the Second Empire, Goncourt (who studied the poorest people as entomologists study insects) recorded one such, commenting:

What is it to me that there should be monuments, opéras, café-concerts, where I have never set foot, because I had no money?

The goals of the Commune were posted up outside the Hôtel de Ville: a municipal budget – local taxation, local control over local education; right of the city to choose its own magistrates, etc., where they were carefully studied by an aristocratic colonel in the Grenadier Guards, the Hon. John C. Stanley, then working with the Red Cross in Paris. This Tory soldier, and ancestor of Nancy Mitford, declared:

I have got into a strong unreasonable sort of sympathy with the best of the Reds. They are fighting for municipal liberties – which all our towns have always enjoyed.

On polling day, the late Emperor, Louis-Napoléon, still captive in Germany, sent a pathetic proclamation, declaring he had been 'betrayed by fortune' and reminding France that he was still its 'real representative' and that any other Government would be 'illegiti-mate'.

On Tuesday 28 March, 1871 – a day of delicious spring sunshine – the Commune installed itself in the Hôtel de Ville. Newly-elected members, wearing red scarves, stood on the scarlet-draped platform before the wildly cheering public, as the National Guard marched by, magnificently by all accounts, with a spring in their step and that swagger which onlookers cherish. Salvoes of cannon-fire pealed from batteries on the quays. All the statues were draped in red. The bust of the République wore a red Phrygian cap, which officers of the National Guard saluted with their sabres.

'*Vive la Commune!*' the crowds roared as the National Guards raised their képis on the points of their bayonets and massed bands thundered out the *Marseillaise*. 'What a day! O great Paris!' cried Jules Vallés.

It was fated to last only seven weeks and end in horror.

Karl Marx, sitting in his spider's web of international intrigue in London, was disturbed. A Commune in Paris was outside his plans altogether, and he regarded it as folly. He still believed that only an educated and enlightened German proletariat could pull it off.

'The International did not raise a finger to initiate the Commune,' Engels put on record.

Whilst struggling for its survival, the Commune, in April and May, set to work on social reforms. Some golden nuggets in a mass of trivia:

DECREES

1. The salaries of Government officials were to be limited to the equivalent of workmen's wages.
2. The rents unpaid during the Siege, which Thiers had ordered to be paid, were to be cancelled.
3. Workshops abandoned by their owners were to be National-ised (but the end came before this could be carried out).
4. Fines imposed on workers were to be abolished.
5. Night baking (a deep grievance) was to be abolished.
6. An attempt was to be made to combat prostitution.
7. Wives (legal or otherwise) and children of men killed defend-ing Paris were to receive pensions.
8. Education to be tackled head on.

9. Courbet to be appointed to get the museums in order and open to the public without delay.

and, of course, the big objective:

10. Autonomy of the Commune.
11. Control of the budget – its services, magistrature, police and education, and the right to introduce whatever reforms were necessary.

Courbet had long been urging that the Vendôme Column – to him the symbol of militarism and imperialism and an artistic eye-sore – should be demolished. 155 feet high, with an immensely thick shaft, it was a copy of Trojan's famous Column, with bronze bas-reliefs cast from melted-down enemy cannon, celebrating Napoléon's 1805 campaign. The original figure at the top had been that of the French Emperor, massive in a toga. When Louis-Philippe took over the throne this statue was replaced by another one of Napoléon in the uniform he had worn at Austerlitz. When Louis-Napoléon took over the throne, Napoléon reappeared on the top of the Column in his Imperial robes.

The technical difficulties of its demolition were considerable. But at last all was ready for the big day (16 May). Special invitation cards to witness the demolition bore a Phrygian cap. Three bands and several battalions of National Guards crammed into the Place Vendôme (now renamed 'Place Internationale'). All the windows in the vicinity were prudently criss-crossed with strips of paper, and 10,000 spectators throbbed with excitement. Colonel Stanley recorded: 'It was black vandalism but, as it was to fall, I would not have missed it for a great deal.'

After a false start, it fell with a mighty crash and a great cloud of dust. The bands played the *Marseillaise* and the crowds rushed to gather bits of plaster and bronze mementoes. Nobody listened to the heroic speeches and roars of: '*Vive la Commune!*'

An American girl, staying with her family in the nearby Hôtel Mirabeau, played *Hail Columbia!* very loudly on the piano in their first-floor suite, and gave an American cheer in which all her family joined.

Time was against the Commune. Thiers was mobilising an army

to destroy it, and the German army of occupation was camped outside the Gates of Paris.

The leaders of the Commune were haggard men who had spent their lives in exile, or in French prisons, or on Devil's Island. They were politicians and journalists, good on fiery speeches and passionate editorials but with no practical experience in administration at all.

To run a great city of two and a half million people you need bankers, engineers, practical economists, civil service experts in all administrative skills and duties. Many mistakes were made. The most serious was to let the Banque de France take all its money away.

Elected members of the City Commune covered every shade of political affiliation from mild liberalism to the extreme left. The oratory was breath-taking, the disputes unceasing, the voting interminable. Precious time was wasted when they should have been consolidating their municipal mandate. Everything that could go wrong did go wrong.

Something of the same preoccupation with visual effects, emotive phrases and dramatic symbols, which had been so cultivated in the Second Empire, seemed to have rubbed off on the Commune.

Shelling from Thiers' guns grew heavier than Bismarck's had been. Thiers' own mansion in the Place St Georges would have been hit by his own shells sooner or later. As it was the Commune saved him the trouble. On 15 May, twenty carts began clearing out the contents. The various treasures were distributed among the city libraries and museums. The linen was sent to the hospitals. Then his house was razed.

Meanwhile, to speed up his plan to conquer Paris, Thiers secretly tried to bribe leading figures in the Commune to sell out for one million francs each.

Pipe-en-Bois (Georges Cavalier), who had organised the claque against Cora at the twelfth performance of *Orphée aux Enfers*, was appointed Engineer-in-Chief of Roads and Public Highways, a job which folded up when the Commune folded up. He escaped.

Nevertheless, the Commune brought some joy back into Paris, for so long grey and hopeless. A hugely popular series of outdoor concerts took place in the gardens of the Tuileries. The theatres were opening again and the popular music-hall singer, Madame Bordas, delighted the vast audiences when she sang: 'C'est la Canaille! Eh bien, j'en suis.'

Barricades were steadily going up to repel Thiers' troops when they should invade (hopefully not for a long time) and shelling from Thiers' cannon was still battering Paris indiscriminately, when on Sunday, 21 May, a huge outdoor concert took place in the Tuileries Gardens. 1,500 musicians played Meyerbeer, Mozart and the great classics. A popular success. A Communard Staff Officer mounted the rostrum at the end, to thank the public for coming and announced:

Citizens! Monsieur Thiers promised to enter Paris yesterday. Monsieur Thiers did not enter. Therefore, I invite you all to come back next Sunday, here at the same place . . .

At that very moment the troops of Monsieur Thiers were beginning to pour into the city.

There followed the most terrible week even Paris had ever experienced. Street by street, house by house, every inch was desperately fought over.

In the elegant quarters of Paris, General MacMahon and his troops were welcomed as deliverers with flowers and Tricolour flags. But in the rest of Paris the fiercest resistance met the invaders. Soldiers who had put up only an indifferent fight against Bismarck's troops during the war, now fought like demons against their fellow citizens.

As the civil war gained in intensity, Cora saw in the anguished faces of Madame Laforêt and Salé that she was a foreigner, a foreigner despite her many years residence and her total commitment to Paris. It was not that her faithful servants did not love her. They did. But Paris, stabbing herself to death, had become totally self-absorbed. She did not want the responsibility of foreigners getting in the way.

So Madame Laforêt, Salé, and the Mother Superior all begged Cora to go back to England, where Plon-Plon was anxious for her to join him in London.

But her hospital? It was almost empty now. At last Cora decided she would go back to England if her staff and Mother Superior Beneventura promised to keep her hospital open for victims of the civil war. Salé announced that he was joining the *Gardes Nationales* to have a bash at Thiers, whom he hated.

Finally, deeply upset, Cora consented to go, leaving the rest of her jewels with the Mother Superior to pay wages and supply her hospital. Madame Laforêt was certain Plon-Plon would return one day and Cora was entrusted with a message for him – that his nightshirt and night-cap were being kept in lavender ready for his homecoming. Plon-Plon instructed Cora to reserve the best suite at London's Grosvenor Hotel for a month and arranged for money to be available for payment in advance.

At last, Madame Laforêt in tears, and Salé pushing Cora's *vélocipède* loaded with her portmanteaux, accompanied Cora to the Gare St Lazarre to see her off.

Cora was now thirty years old, no longer an impudent laughing girl with a rosy complexion and incredible jewels. She was thinner, more serious; adult at last. Or so she appeared to be.

In perfect sunny weather the carnage in Paris increased. Retreating Communards fired a building behind them to hold back Thiers' troops. Soon, buildings were blazing wherever the fighting was fiercest. Pails of water and handpumps were futile. From England Gladstone offered fire-engines.

Lord Lyons, the British Ambassador, had left the British Embassy in Paris in charge of Edward Malet, who resisted the demand of one of Thiers' Colonels to take it over completely. But he agreed to allow the Embassy dining room to be turned into an *ambulance*, and mattresses were spread over the Embassy dining table ready for the wounded. Malet was now obliged to dine in his own cellar, which was crammed with Embassy treasures and strong-boxes. There he sat, in full evening dress, waited upon by the Embassy butler and footmen in full livery, listening to the crump of cannon and the roaring of flames outside. There was a notice from the Siege, still hanging on the wall:

BRITISH SUBJECTS WHO CONTINUE TO REMAIN IN PARIS NOW, DO SO AT THEIR OWN RISK AND PERIL.

Against a radiant night sky the incendiarism increased, an awesome spectacle like a vision of hell; the Tuileries ablaze, the Hôtel de Ville ablaze, the Louvre ablaze. The weather, which had played such an important rôle in Paris politics, now joined in again with a fierce wind which fanned the destructive flames.

Civil war destroys without discrimination. There were too many firearms about – too much petrol available. What should have been the people's inheritance, went up in flames.

The bitterest fighting took place in the slums of Belleville and Mélimontant. Then Thiers sent his troops into Montmartre to take by force the two hundred precious cannon which the people refused to surrender.

Louise Michel, always where the battle was fiercest, rushed down the hill waving her rifle above her head, shouting 'Treason!'

Even at this stage of the war the fecklessness of the French officers once again revealed itself. The officer in charge of the operation, having seized the two hundred cannon, was unable to carry them away because he had forgotten to bring horses for their transport. So the two hundred cannon had the last grisly laugh and stayed where they were.

When the Père-Lachaise cemetery was shattered in one of the fiercest battles of this civil war, the handsome marble monument erected to the memory of the Duc de Morny was damaged, the Communard cannon firing its final round from its shelter before the hand-to-hand combat.

On 29 May 1871, *The Times* reported:

The laws of war! They are mild and Christian compared with the inhuman laws of revenge under which the Versailles troops have been shooting, bayonetting, ripping up prisoners, women and children, during the last six days. So far as we can recollect there has been nothing like it in history . . .

Louise Michel, amazingly unhurt though everywhere in the thick of the fighting, sought refuge with a friend when the fighting ceased. Then she went in search of her mother. Learning that her mother had been seized as a hostage for herself, Louise gave herself up to save the old lady's life. At her trial in Versailles her defiant spirit impressed the Court:

I wanted to oppose the Versailles invaders with a barrier of flames! – I want to die with my friends and, if you let me live, I shall never cease to cry Vengeance!

She was sentenced to life imprisonment in the penal colony of Noumea – another Devil's Island.

Renoir, the marvellous painter of the marvels of the ordinary, must have the last word about the Commune he had lived through: 'They were madmen. But they had in them that little flame which never dies.'

14
England

Once Cora had left Paris, the quiet of the countryside amazed her. She stared at the fields of vegetables the farmers had feared to take into Paris. Cora had forgotten the sound of silence. Since she had opened her hospital she had never known an unbroken night, only the noise of the gunfire and shells bursting overhead.

On the Channel crossing she slept; too tired to think. What was she letting herself in for? Best not to plan anything, not to worry about the future. She had done exactly what Plon-Plon had asked – booked the best suite at the Grosvenor Hotel in the name of the Count and Countess Jérome, and paid a month in advance.

Plon-Plon was probably in Italy seeing what money he could raise. Like all royalty out of work, he travelled under a variety of names, booking into Grand Hotels as the Duke of this and the Count of that. At least Jérome was his father's name and not difficult for English people to pronounce.

Cora realized suddenly that her cockney French would do her no good in England. She must remember to speak the careful French she had been taught and had so successfully rejected at her Boulogne convent school so long ago. And she must not forget to speak lady-like English, as her parents had insisted. Her mother was living in London. But Cora must not try to see her. It would only cause a scandal.

With nothing left of her own (home gone, jewels gone, horses far away) Cora would have to give up her dear, darling independence. But there was no alternative. Plon-Plon would be much changed.

His habitual sour melancholy, which only she could soften, must be worsened by the disasters which had overtaken France. Well, she would try to cheer him up and entertain him. Cora did not feel like entertaining anybody just now. She felt she needed comfort herself.

Then her innate courage took over. When she had unpacked and rested she would be her merry, witty self again. But her thoughts kept drifting to her beloved horses – so far away. They were her real family. Of course she was fond of Gustave Doré, last heard of on the ramparts of Paris with rifle and sketchbook. Where was he now?

In fact Doré had made a series of invaluable drawings of everything round him during the Siege; but he resisted all temptations to show them in London, where he had his own gallery, because they gave such a haunting account of France in her humiliation and Doré loved France passionately. He did manage to get his mother to Versailles and safety when the Siege ended. But he found the 'pomposity and idiocy' of Thiers' Government there so obnoxious that he drew a series of biting cartoons of it, including a telling caricature of Thiers himself.

Caroline Hassé and Caroline Letessier, Cora learned, had escaped to England. But, in prudish England, how would they earn their living, the only one they knew, when their English clients had always come over to France to escape from England?

Nostalgia overwhelmed Cora as she remembered one specially delightful summer weekend at Beauséjour with Morny and Doré and *la bande*, when they had all danced crazily to Offenbach's absurd *Valse de la Basse-cour*, with its musical mooing of cows, cackling of hens and grunting of pigs. And how she had waltzed elegantly on her green lawn with Emmanuel, her pet piglet. All gone! All gone forever!

Cora was soberly dressed in a pre-war travelling cloak and hat (made by Worth, naturally), with no make-up and no jewellery. No-one would recognize her in London surely.

The train puffed noisily into Victoria Station. A horde of sturdy obsequious porters – so different from the haggard independent starvelings of the Gare St Lazarre – descended on her portmanteaux and followed her into the Grosvenor Hotel. It is still there and architecturally little changed; huge rooms, lofty ceilings and long corridors.

The Manager hurried to receive her, bowing very low. Yes, the suite reserved for the Count and Countess, the best in the Hotel, awaited her. Everything would be done to make her comfortable. All her requirements would be instantly attended to. The Countess had only to touch the bell . . . A personal maid was waiting, if required . . . Understandably, in view of the tragic happenings in Paris, the Countess had not brought her personal maid with her. Tea, comforting strong British tea, would be sent to her suite at once. And there was a hot-water-bottle in her bed. The Count had communicated to announce his return to England very soon.

And here, having arrived at the best suite, the Manager unlocked the massive mahogany door and, bowing double, indicated the huge bouquet Plon-Plon had ordered to be waiting for her.

Cora examined the best suite curiously before she took off her travelling cloak. The huge sitting room was furnished with massive armchairs and a sofa upholstered in dark green rep with stiffly-starched anti-macassars. The wallpaper was a dark green. There was a grand piano covered with a heavy fringed, plush cloth to match. On the wall above the fireplace hung an enormous steel engraving of the widowed Queen Victoria in her widow's peaked cap. The bedroom was furnished *en suite*; Plon-Plon's dressing room the same, only slightly smaller; the bathroom (no bidet, of course) very large, very cold, with icy white towels and a view over the station.

Her cold sponge-down every morning (such a pleasure in her warm, perfumed bathroom in her rue de Chaillot mansion) would be a penance in this puritanical bathroom. But never mind. It would not be for long. Four weeks only.

The tea arrived in a massive silver teapot, with hot buttered muffins and generous slices of richly curranted plum cake. Cora sat with her feet on a footstool covered with plush to match the curtains.

So she was back in England – her England. Why then did she feel so utterly alien here? A foreigner. She had felt more at home during the shelling and bombarding of Paris in an alien war, than in this icy British mausoleum.

During all her years in Paris, Cora had upheld her Englishness, speaking French with a cockney accent to underline her nationality. She had always sent to Covent Garden for her 'slap' and all her cosmetics, her hair-washes and hair-dyes. She had always ordered Axminster and Wilton carpets from England for her houses. She had employed only English grooms and subscribed only to English charities.

Now here she was back in England, but it was no longer the England she imagined. She had been seeing England for years through the admiring, jealous French eyes of her clients. The England she thus had seen was the England of the aristocracy: the Jockey Club, the House of Lords, the great country estates, whose owners came to Paris to frolic, the upper-crust England of splendid horses, stately homes, well-bred dogs and careless noblemen.

What she was seeing now was entrenched middle-class England; solid, respectable, hard-faced, middle-class England, which abhored luxury and was very prudent indeed in money matters. She had never seen it before and she did not like it.

Cora went to bed early, her heart homing back to Madame Laforêt in rue Chaillot and Salé. And she went to sleep thinking of her beloved horses at Cabourg and resolved to get Plon–Plon away from London and into the country as soon as possible.

During the next few days Cora rested, slept and wrote letters. She did not know whether her letters would ever be delivered, in the chaos and disorganisation that then was Paris.

The day Plon-Plon was expected, the manager tapped on the door of her apartment and entered abruptly. He was in a state of consternation and could hardly bring himself to speak. At last he got the words out: 'Madame, I have been informed that you are none other than Cora Pearl.' Cora smiled graciously. She had been accustomed to adulation for years. She observed a lubricious gleam in his eyes. She had often seen it before in the eyes of respectable men. The manager had gone red in the face and looked as though he were about to throw an apoplectic fit. He thundered:'Madame, this is a respectable family hotel. You must leave at once!' As always, in a difficult situation, Cora hardened. She replied coldly: 'You have been paid a month in advance.' The manager thundered from behind his stiff collar: 'You must leave at once and there will be no refund.'

At this moment, Plon-Plon, his arms full of flowers and bon-bons, burst into the room, his saturnine face beaming with joy at the sight of his *Perle bien-aimée*.

Cora explained the situation. Plon-Plon flew into a furious rage, cursing the wretched manager with a torrent of oaths so obscene that Cora was relieved the manager did not understand French, then following this up shouting in English that he would blacken the Grosvenor's reputation everywhere. The manager fled.

Cora, calm and smiling, continued her *maquillage*, which the manager had interrupted, as she waited for Plon-Plon's rage to subside. The question was, where should they go? Claridges? Plon-Plon would not hear of it. It was full of swaggering German officers. The Carlton? No, they were there too. Well then, the Ritz? Their portmanteaux followed them to the Ritz.

However, Cora soon found a commodious house to rent in Sussex, where the hunting was excellent, and there they went. Plon-Plon, who was trying to be careful with his dwindling resources, had to pay £1,000 for five weeks' rental, an enormous sum.

'Well, Plon-Plon, this is England – we cannot expect Meudon or Beauséjour – so let's make the best of it,' cajoled Cora, as appalled as Plon-Plon by the heavy furniture, the scratchy horsehair chairs in the dining room, the heavy plush curtains (dark red this time), the 'good plain cook' and the tight-lipped housekeeper. Also, of course, the obligatory widowed Queen glaring at them from her engraved portrait, in the sitting room.

Plon-Plon, to avoid further unpleasantness, had begged Cora to wear a wedding-ring. She could not bear 'such a bondage', so she compromised by wearing a band of gilt paper, which she took off every night before she jumped into the awesome matrimonial bed.

Plon-Plon, as she had predicted, was in a state of deep gloom. He pored over the newspapers all day, as the news from France worsened by the hour. Cora vainly tried her best to distract him. He was her 'protector'. But now it was she who was protecting him. He had become sorry for himself; a man of outstanding ability and intelligence, never given a chance of fulfilling himself . . . and so on. He cursed his fate which had ordained that he should be born with an engraved silver spoon in his mouth, plus an elder brother. Cora pointed out that it was worse to be born, as she had been, with no spoon at all in her mouth, but that had not stopped her from making a career for herself.

Plon-Plon, who had a high opinion of Cora's ability and intelligence, told her that she could have been another Florence Nightingale, if only . . . But Cora had no patience with 'if onlys'. Florence Nightingale, she reminded him sharply, came from a wealthy and influential family. There were no opportunities in England for poor unprivileged girls to make a respectable career for themselves . . . except maybe as a lady missionary – and Cora laughed till she cried at the idea of herself as a lady missionary, then Plon-Plon laughed too. 'Let us live and enjoy life while we can!' she cried, wiping her eyes. 'There's excellent hunting in Sussex.'

So Cora joined the Southdown Foxhounds. Plon-Plon bought her a fine mount, and she was soon in excellent health and high spirits again. If one or two gentlemen riders with the hunt recognised Cora, they were discreet enough not to let on.

Brighton was fun. It had retained something of its Regency rakishness. They stayed at the comfortable Grand Hotel and watched the sun set over the shimmering sea as they drank champagne on the terrace. Cora loved the Brighton Pavilion, a pantomime extravaganza in cast iron and stained glass. Queen Victoria had sold it to the Brighton Borough Council, being anxious to dissociate herself from Prinny's rakish image, and the Council had hastily covered the authentic Chinese wallpapers with dark-brown and dark-green municipal paint. And so it remained until, after the Second World War, the brilliant new director, Clifford Musgrave, resolved to bring this very British Chinese Pavilion back to its former glory, and spent the rest of his life doing so.

Plon-Plon, whose restlessness increased with the realization that he could never return to France, took Cora on aimless travels. Their one successful jaunt was to Dublin, where Plon-Plon was too well-known as Prince Napoléon to call himself anything else. The Mayor of Dublin laid on a grand municipal reception, innocently assuming Cora to be the Princess Clothilde. Cora put up a brave show, playing the gracious confident princess poor Clothilde never was and never could be. Horse-mad Dublin was enchanted with Cora's equestrian skill.

Time and money slipped away fast. The Commune had been defeated. Paris, now under Thiers' iron heel, was licking its wounds and, with the rest of France, making agonizing economies to pay off the five thousand million francs war indemnity. Amazingly, they achieved this quickly, paying the first half after a month and the rest by September 1873. It was like scrubbing their Paris pavements with

Condy's fluid after the Prussian March of Triumph. They wanted to be rid of anything to do with their humiliation.

Cora's friends, Caroline Hassé and Caroline Letessier, now in England 'looking for work', decided to go to Oxford to trace a certain young undergraduate with whom they had once frolicked in Paris. They were broke – he had always been kind. Surely he would introduce them to some of his well-heeled friends in need of their services.

They booked in at the Randolph Hotel and tracked down the undergraduate in his college. Petrified with embarrassment, he implored them to remove all their cosmetics and to behave like noble ladies ruined by the Commune. Then he took them to call on Dr Liddell, the Dean of Christchurch, and his wife, whose second daughter was the Alice Lewis Carrol immortalised in *Alice in Wonderland*. The two Carolines touched the hearts of the Liddells who invited them home for tea and croquet with their daughters.

But this wasn't getting the two Carolines very far, and presently they took tender leave of the saintly Liddells and pretty little Alice, and fled back to London to the more profitable hunting grounds of the Cremorne Gardens.

Plon-Plon now advised Cora to return to Paris to retrieve what assets she had left. They were considerable. There was her mansion in rue de Chaillot, damaged no doubt, but worth a considerable sum, besides her collection of silver, her precious bibelots, her valuable furniture – and that other mansion he had given her in the rue des Bassins; all indisputably hers. (Knowing his Cora so well, he was sure she had kept all the title deeds neatly filed.) And then there was the Château de Beauséjour . . . But here Cora stopped him, really upset for once. She would never, never sell her beloved Beauséjour, where she intended to end her days peacefully with her horses and her dogs . . . anyway, she reminded him, it was heavily mortgaged.

Plon-Plon, who loved Cora in his curious way, promised to send her money whenever he could, and planned that they should meet – sometime, somewhere, somehow. He would keep in touch and send her little presents. And, for her part, Cora must be *sage*, not get herself into trouble, and she must watch her diet. He was proud of Cora's beautiful figure and believed soup was bad for her.

So, after a liaison of six years, they parted. Cora, glad to be independent once more, though she was fond of Plon-Plon in her curious way, crossed the Channel to start again.

Now she was into her thirties. She must put her affairs in order. High time too.

15
Duval

She was warmly welcomed back by Madame Laforêt, Salé, and her friend the Mother Superior Beneventura. Her hospital-home in the rue de Chaillot had been considerably damaged in the bombardment and civil war. It was spotlessly clean but very shabby. Her once pretty garden was desolate. Madame Laforêt had aged considerably and Salé, having lost a leg in the fighting, now stumped about on crutches, boisterous as ever. Mother Beneventura had wound up the hospital when the Commune ended and their last patient had gone – cured or dead. There were debts to pay off, and she handed Cora a sheaf of bills, all in perfect order.

She told Cora that Thiers' new Government (anxious to kindle pride in the citizens of Paris he had helped to destroy), were now patriotically recompensing those who had turned their homes into *ambulances* during the Siege, by awarding them Diplomas of Honour and refunds of outlay. She advised Cora to apply. Cora did so, the Mother Superior strongly endorsing her application.

Cora's business-like application was ignored. Thinking that there must have been an administrative muddle, Cora tried again. This time there was no mistake. It was a deliberate rebuff. Cora was deeply hurt. The Mother Superior was outraged and stopped brooding over the loss of her beloved Lorraine to say exactly what she thought about the spiteful Government. She knew very well that Cora badly needed the compensation money. The Mother Superior had sold Cora's jewels to the best of her shrewd ability, but they hadn't brought in as much as they were worth, and the *ambulance* had swallowed that up like lightning.

Cora felt that it was not only herself whom the Government was insulting but her dear *mobiles* too. Her memoirs tell the story in her own strong language: 'I was not even offered a Diploma. I am not complaining in anger but simply stating a fact.' She had (she recounts) spent 25,000 francs on her small hospital (certainly she had spent far more) and she had only claimed 15,000 francs. And she needed the money badly or she would not have applied.

It was the hypocrisy that angered Cora. She got over her indignation eventually (after she had taken her case to the tribunal, only to be awarded an insultingly derisory hand-out).

If I had my time over again, [she recorded in her memoirs, wiser, perhaps even mellowed by the passage of painful years] I would not appeal to Justice – a lot of trouble for nothing! I would rather take things cheerfully in my stride. There are things one does in good faith not worth doing for the bad blood they cause . . . A Diploma! Bah! What a farce! The finest diploma is the recognition of the common people . . .

Her *moblots* showed the most touching gratitude and never forgot her.

But Cora had once again tangled with French authorities. A little bell should have tinkled warningly to remind her not to do so. The French authorities had her on their list. England and the English were now again out of favour in France.

Cora's two grooms returned from Cabourg with her eight horses in excellent condition, and a batch of bills. The money and jewels Cora had left them had not sufficed, the jewels not realizing anything like their true value on the topsy-turvy market. Her grooms informed her that Lord Derby wanted to buy her eight horses and employ their two grooms to look after them. He had made a generous offer and, of course, they would become part of the finest stables in England. What did Madame wish?

Cora had to let them go. She felt orphaned without them but she needed the money desperately. Salé, boisterous as a schoolboy, now proposed a little conference *à trois* in Madame Cora's boudoir, so that they could take stock of the situation. He clattered off on his crutches to prepare an omelette, whilst Madame Laforêt set a meticulous table – one of Cora's delicious little nonsense tables meant for a much more frivolous conference.

It cheered Cora tremendously to hear old Salé banging about and whistling in the kitchen as in the old days, when he had always had the services of a full-time assistant cook and a kitchen maid. Now he did everything himself, even managing to scrub the kitchen floor on his crutches.

'Now,' said Cora briskly, the omelette consumed and the three of them drinking their coffee, 'Money! What shall we do for money? I must get a rich lover without delay – the richer the better.'

But this was not going to be easy, they explained to her. The foreign princes and South American millionaires who had fled from the Siege had never returned. What was there to return to? Paris was burnt out, penny-pinching and puritanical. All the well-known courtesans had dispersed to Monte Carlo, Monaco, Baden, following their clients. Everything – fashion, the theatre, the famous restaurants, had folded up. Paris was *foutu*!

Even philanthropist Richard Wallace, whom the French Government had honoured for his generosity, had packed up his incomparable art collection and gone to settle in London after the final donation of a million francs for the relief of the Paris poor, to include the erection of a, hopefully, hygienic drinking fountain. With him gone, Salé pointed out, the cult of Britannia was absolutely finished.

Cora refused to be depressed. No! No! Surely there must be at least *one* rich man left in Paris. Salé and Madame Laforêt exchanged a look of embarrassment. 'Out with it!' cried Cora, 'You *do* know of such a man. No doubt he is odious. Never mind that! The important thing is that he must be rich . . .'

There was indeed such a young man – very rich; absolutely odious. Not in Cora's class at all, but . . . 'Get him,' ordered Cora, 'as soon as possible. By the way, what is his name?'

His name was Duval, Alexandre Duval. His age was twenty-seven. He was the spoiled son of a small horse-meat butcher who had made an enormous fortune from a chain of cheap eating-houses. *Bouillon et Boeuf*, serving a large plateful for the equivalent of ten pence, or just soup for the equivalent of two-and-a-half pence and, posh touch, a paper tablecloth, if required, for an extra half penny. The successful father had left ten million francs on his death, and his devoted wife had then devoted herself to spoiling their only son, Alexandre, who was reputed to be of a hysterical and romantic nature, cultivating a nostalgia for the Second Empire which he had missed. Not Cora's cup of tea at all. But needs must.

Cora was already planning what to do with the Duval millions: pay the accumulated bills; engage new staff to assist Madame Laforêt and Salé; buy new carpets, new furniture, new bibelots, new clothes, new jewels, another stable of fine horses . . . and give gorgeous dinner parties and fabulous balls again. For Cora could not, would not understand that the dizzy days of the Second Empire were gone forever. Cora was all for having a go again. Duval had the money. She had the know-how.

In due course a rendezvous was arranged. Cora, dressed in a pre-war Worth gown, discreetly made-up, her red curls carefully arranged, wearing no jewels because she had none left, received young Duval in her shabby but still elegant salon beneath her equestrian portrait. Duval, speechless with nervous anticipation, presented Cora with a huge vulgar bouquet and a lavishly bound album.

Cora explained to him her code of conduct:

1. No money. No favours.
2. When the liaison was over – and it was she who would decide when it was over – then it was over.

Duval fell on his knees and stammered conventional compliments, begging her to examine the album. Cora opened it. Every leaf was a thousand-franc banknote and there were one hundred leaves. Not a bad start.

At this moment, Madame Laforêt tiptoed in, carrying Plon-Plon's starched nightshirt and nightcap on a silver tray, the Napoléonic bees and eagles clearly visible. 'Would Monsieur,' asked Madame Laforêt in her gentle, well-bred voice, 'be requiring these?'

Duval had no sense of humour, no *savoir-faire*. He was a bore. But he picked up the bills and became daily more infatuated, Cora held the key to his social ambitions. She had been the mistress of the legendary Duc de Morny, the King of the Jockey Club and the most famous *boulevardier* of them all. Surely what had rubbed off on Cora must now rub off on Alexandre Duval.

Cora threw herself into the refurbishing of her rue de Chaillot home. She ordered from England a magnificent yellow Axminster carpet to be specially woven for her. She bought costly replacements of china and furniture, new clothes, new jewels. She engaged more staff. When the ex-Emperor's famous stable of horses came onto the market Cora successfully bid for several of them. And Duval paid all the bills without a word of complaint.

Then, one day, Duval, looking hang-dog, came to see her. When Cora presented him with her latest batch of bills he confessed tearfully that he was unable to pay them. His mother, who controlled his money, had withdrawn his allowance and was stopping all his cheques. In fact his doting mother was seriously considering confining him to a lunatic asylum, before Cora gobbled up all the family fortune.

Cora did not turn a hair. 'You know my rules Monsieur Duval: No money – no favours. I bid you good-bye.'

Madame Laforêt politely escorted Duval out. She reported to Cora that he had a wild look in his eyes, like an angry baby. Later that evening Duval returned and hammered on the front door. The staff had orders not to admit him. The next day he returned again, banging on the front door, shrieking for admittance. On the third it rained. Duval had now worked himself up into a romantic frenzy and was resolved to shoot Cora.

On the morning of 19 December 1871 (a rainy day), Duval's concierge found him cleaning and oiling his revolvers and took them away from him. But he found where she had hidden them, and set off in the rain on his mission. On the way he stopped at the barber's to have his hair and moustaches shampooed and curled. Once again he stood outside Cora's front door, where Salé had taken over from the frightened housemaids. This time he managed to break in.

Duval then rushed into the salon and confronted Cora, waving his revolver, screaming he was going to kill her. Cora kept cool, telling him not to behave like a silly child but to put down the revolver at once and pull himself together. Cora had no idea the revolver was loaded, nor that Duval's performance was anything but a silly practical joke.

Duval, who had pointed the revolver at Cora, now hysterically turned it on himself and fired, collapsing on Cora's new yellow carpet in a pool of blood. The bullet had entered his left lung and lodged in his back. Two doctors and a surgeon were sent for urgently. Journalists and press photographers rushed in and filled the house. Duval, losing a lot of blood through his mouth, was still conscious. The doctors had Duval carried to a bedroom on the second floor. They did not expect him to live. The police arrived and hustled Cora off to the police station. The doctors ordered Duval's mother to be sent for; Madame Duval arrived in a state of frenzy and added her lamentations to the uproar.

Though Madame Duval hated Cora, who had taken her son from her, this respectable woman could not resist having a prurient stare round Cora's house, especially at her bathroom of rose marble with her monogram engraved in gold on the luxurious bath-tub.

For days Duval lay in a desperate condition, the newspapers, in their almost hourly bulletins, referring to him as 'the moribund'. He spoke occasionally – the eager journalists scribbling down every word. Once he said in a tragic voice that he had killed himself to prove his love.

But (to look ahead) Duval was not dying after all. Before long he had recovered sufficiently to be removed to his own establishment to be properly nursed. He ordered all the newspapers and had all the press articles about himself read aloud to him. Daily Duval grew stronger and finally, in March 1873, only three months after the shooting, he was seen in a box at the Vaudeville enjoying a satirical song about the scandal, in which he was referred to as: '*un jeune sybarite aux long cheveux gommés.*' And when the audience rocked with laughter and pointed to him in his box, he stood up, smiled and nodded. Duval had not learned to be a *boulevardier*, but he had certainly achieved notoriety.

Cora, hustled to the police station, through the rain-swept streets, where crowds jeered and spat at her, had not been given time even to snatch a coat. Inside the police station Cora was coldly informed that if Duval died she would go to the guillotine as his murderess. (For Thiers had restored the guillotine which the Commune had abolished.)

Cora realized she was in a very bad situation. She had been alone with Duval when he had pulled the trigger – therefore no witnesses. What she needed desperately was a good lawyer. When at last Madame Laforêt managed to push through the shouting mob and get to Cora, guarded by two surly policemen, Cora begged her to get hold of her lawyer at once.

Madame Laforêt, leaving her own shawl to protect Cora, hurried off to do so. When the police had taken Cora away Salé was left to cope with the flood of journalists and press artists and photographers who had invaded the house and were scribbling reports and photographing and sketching the blood-stained carpet, the terrified housemaids and tearful Madame Duval. One wily press photographer managed to slip upstairs and photograph 'the moribund' himself. They even fingered the fatal revolver until a frantic gendarme threw them all out.

Headlines in all the papers all over Europe reported: 'The biggest scandal of the Year.' Foreign correspondents had a field day.

Meanwhile, at the police station, Cora had been interrogated by the Chief of Police himself, Monsieur Patinot: 'Why were there no witnesses to the shooting?' (her mansion was full of servants at the time). 'The prisoner maintains Alexandre Duval shot himself,' . . . ridiculous! The only child of the late public benefactor, restaurateur Duval, young Alexandre – the sole comfort of his bereaved mother – had everything to live for: joy, hope, ambition. He was of tender years (in fact he was only three years younger than Cora) whereas Mademoiselle Cora Pearl, the prisoner, was a notorious *femme publique* with a bad record – besides being an alien Englishwoman. She must have had a good reason for quitting herself of the young man she had ruined and now wished to rid herself of . . . and so on.

Cora's lawyer, Maître Lefoullon, had arrived to help. Everything, he explained to her, depended on whether Duval lived or died. In the current emotional climate in France, all foreigners were distrusted. No Frenchman was going to believe Cora's account of the shooting. She must not expect justice. Meanwhile he would prudently see that some of Cora's treasures were transferred to a safe place. Cora listed a few she cared for, including her equestrian portrait, her Durer painting and the gold Doré goblet made for Morny. She sent, via Maître Lefoullon, a private word to Madame Laforêt, asking her to take into her personal care Cora's important private ledger which listed all details of her professional life (clients, earnings, dates and comments), and keep it under lock and key. What the newspapers would have made out of that! Fortunately, they never found it.

Monsieur Patinot grilled her every day. Cora stuck to her story: Duval had been her lover. She had given him his *congé*. When she accepted him as her lover he had accepted her terms. It was he who was breaking those terms. Yes, his mother, Madame Duval, had been bitterly opposed to the liaison.

Interrogated about Alexandre, Cora declared he was of a hysterical nature and emotionally immature. She did not deny that her profession was that of courtesan. Her clients had included some of the highest in the land.

She had never before had trouble of this kind; her clients, she pointed out, all being of a superior class. All this, with lurid comments, appeared every day in every French newspaper and many foreign ones. Wherever he was, Plon-Plon must have seen them.

Cora was horrified and bewildered by the spite and vindictiveness of the newspapers which so recently had flattered and fawned on her. The truth was that Thiers kept as tight a stranglehold on the French press as had Louis-Napoléon. The journalists were glad of a scandal to provide juicy copy. While the public gloated over their revelations, condemning Cora as a heartless whore and an alien Englishwoman, the middle-aged gentlemen at the Jockey Club (Duval's unattainable goal), talked over Cora's plight, stroking their imperials – faithfully styled after de Morny – agreeing that Cora had been tactless but absolutely right. No gentleman would have broken Cora's terms. No gentleman would have made embarrassing scenes. Duval was an upstart – a *nouveau-riche*.

The Jockey Club was distressed for Cora but powerless to help her. Maître Lefoullon had not called on them to testify to her good character. Cora did not have a good character. And the Jockey Club itself was *non grata* under Thiers' dreary Government, where fun was frowned on. Patinot, they felt sure, would get Cora banished from Paris. He would seize her estates and flog their contents in the name of the law. For old times sake, they vowed to attend the auctions and buy back some of her treasures to keep for her. She had always been gay and generous and provided them with unlimited fun. They had kept a tender spot for her. 'No French Government lasts for long. One day Cora will return to Paris,' they declared.

Maître Lefoullon meanwhile had tracked down a French law which ruled that an alien who owned property in France could not be banished from France. Cora was, at least, now saved from deportation.

But Patinot had been doing his own investigations. It was Cora's bad luck that whilst the flames which ended the Commune had destroyed the Tuileries, the library of the Louvre and so much else, the police files had escaped. Patinot had enough evidence to accuse Cora of being an inveterate trouble-maker. He cited three instances: the Court case in 1866 when she was fined for bullying a French child; another Court case in 1864 when she brought a case against her milliner for over-charging and won a rebate on a bill; and, most serious, she had played an offensive practical joke against a high French civic official, before witnesses. On this occasion the Chief of Police himself had warned her that she merited expulsion from France and would be shown no mercy if she misbehaved again.

These previous encounters with the law, aggravated by Cora's scandalous adventure at the now banned Bouffes Theatre, and culminating in the dreadful Duval affair, determined Monsieur Patinot to expel Cora from Paris. He felt, as the evidence accumulated, that the law itself was not emerging from the case too well. Cora, it became clear, had been telling the truth all the time. The evidence of Duval's concierge, plus Duval's own confession that he had shot himself with his own revolver on 19 December, exonerated Cora. The melodrama was turning into a Vaudeville farce. The newspapers were hanging on to the Duval story. Best get Cora out of Paris as soon as possible. Patinot could not legally seize Cora's two mansions, but he could seize and sell their contents to pay her debts. This he determined to do.

Expulsion from Paris in Cora's eyes was worse than exile from France. She went three times to Alexandre's establishment, determined to force him to influence Patinot in her favour. Twice the servants kept her out. The third time she was confronted by Madame Duval herself. Cora put her case to Madame Duval.

According to the *Journal de Paris*, which missed no moment of the Duval melodrama:

Madame Duval, already suffering terribly and hardly recovered from shock, felt ill and had an attack of hysterics, while the servants chased away Mademoiselle Pearl.

So Cora left Paris, pursued by venomous articles in the popular press. One example, the *Petit Journal*, declared:

Never, perhaps, has one of these creatures pushed cynicism to such lengths as Mlle Cora Pearl, an Englishwoman of whom Paris will be rid with no regrets.

To substantiate her claim to her own property in France, Cora had needed to prove her identity. She had the deeds to Beauséjour and her mansions in rue de Chaillot and rue des Bassins. She also owned a small estate at Maisons Lafitte, which the Duc de Rivoli had given her. But how to prove she was Cora Pearl?

She had appealed for help to the British Embassy (which was just as keen to keep her out of England – where the Duval affair had been widely reported – as Cora was to stay in France). She produced a copy of a birth certificate dated 1842 (probably obtained for her by Plon-Plon from Somerset House) which was made out in the name of Cora's younger sister, Louisa Elizabeth, for when Cora was born there were no birth certificates. Cora had already rather clumsily altered the name and the date. It is curious that two of Professor Crouch's daughters should both have been named Elizabeth.

The British Embassy accepted the forgery or, if you prefer, connived at it, and so enabled Cora to claim ownership of her properties and not be expelled from France. And they gave her a proper passport in her real name: Emma Elizabeth Crouch.

Where to go? Cora's name was blackened in every newspaper in Europe, not interested in her acquittal, only in the scandal. Cora decided (a bold stroke, typical of her thinking under stress), to travel briefly back to London to throw the journalists off the scent. Cora booked a modest single room in the Grosvenor Hotel in her own name, Emma Elizabeth Crouch, using it for the first time since 1855. No-one looked twice at her.

Satisfied that she had dodged the press, she returned to France to go to Monaco. But Madame Laforêt warned her that the journalists were on the look-out for her, so Cora repacked her bags and travelled instead to Nice where her old friend Caroline Letessier welcomed her. Caroline, on her return from England, had struck lucky and was being kept in style by the Prince of Monaco's son.

Cora, who had her living to earn, was now ready to continue her professional career. But the French police, determined to destroy her, had warned the police authorities in Nice, Monaco, Monte Carlo and all the other pleasure resorts, that she was an undesirable alien who should not be granted asylum.

The press, which had been so instrumental in making Cora famous, now committed itself to making her infamous. From now on Cora, who so loved putting down roots, was forced to live a vagabond life.

Plon-Plon who, like most dislodged royalties, lived the life of a wandering Jew, carrying with him his bits and pieces, in his case shares, valuable pictures, saleable jewellery, kept in touch with Cora. He had been obliged to sell his treasures at Christies and could not send her much money, nor that often. He was on Cora's side in the Duval affair and horrified at the attacks on her in the European press. Like two wandering stars, very occasionally their orbits met. Under assumed names they snatched a few days together.

The excitement in Paris now centred on the public auction of the contents of Cora's houses. It was an occasion for snide jokes and virtuous head-shaking. The *Journal de Paris* sniggered: 'Any of the givers who are not ruined may repurchase these precious mementoes . . .' Any money remaining, after Cora's debts had been paid off, would go to the State.

Amongst the items listed for sale were: 'A fine white marble statue of Apollo (a present from an Imperial Prince) . . . A massive silver statue given in 1867 by a King . . . Furniture listed as "of unforgettable luxury," ' and, of course, her enormous mahogany bed decorated with columns and gilded figures. Under such unpropitious conditions the sale only realized £14,387.14s. The greatest interest, predictably, was shown in Cora's yellow Axminster carpet because of the large bloodstain.

Cora, wrenched from Paris, living the life of a wanderer, sold her rue de Chaillot house, empty of everything after the auction, to her friend Blanche d'Antigny. Courtesan daughter of a village carpenter, Blanche's life had been even more exciting and tempestuous than Cora's. Perhaps it was an unlucky piece of real estate, for soon after purchasing it, poor Blanche was made bankrupt and fled from her creditors to Cairo where she contracted smallpox and died in Paris aged only thirty-six. Cora grieved for her.

Plon-Plon continued to write cosy little letters trying to fix short get-togethers. One from Rome read:

You know that there is first-class fox-hunting in Rome. As you like little dogs the one I have here is a delicious little creature. Answer this letter. That always gives me great pleasure. Besides, your notepaper carries your scent. If we could only have a few days of pleasure and forgetfulness, it would be good . . .

The following day another letter:

I love you very sincerely. Please believe I could not be cold to you. I have to restrain myself in order not to hasten more than I ought, to go and embrace my dear darling Pearl . . .

Two months later:

I send you the little diamond buckles you wanted and I think it is disinterested on my part to help make you pretty without any gain to myself . . .

And so on. He was over fifty at the time.

In her memoirs the only person Cora calls by his real name is Duval. It would have been foolish to do otherwise as the scandal was too well-known. Cora, whose life he ruined, wrote with dignity and restraint of the affair:

The hero of this adventure being now married and head of an important business, I will simply recall what for such a long time filled the newspapers and even the Revues in the little theatres. Briefly – 'the affair Duval'. I am obliged to mention it because the day after he wounded himself a Police Commissioner called on me with an expulsion order to get out of France. I had to obey. It was a high price to pay for a moment of aberration on the part of another, whom I was very far from having pushed into this act.

Cora's enforced wanderings make painful reading. Time and again she was betrayed to the press by 'friends', by servants, by hoteliers who kept her advance rent. Not only the press but the authorities drove her out. She was always looking for somewhere 'where I might hope to live very quietly so long as I did not go out.'

Nice, Monte Carlo, Monaco – pleasure resorts where she had once frolicked, now all turned against her. Poison-pen letters written by total strangers followed her. 'Misfortune,' recorded Cora in her memoirs, 'pursued me with touching perseverence.'

Cora worked out a stratagem to fox the police. In her memoirs she wrote:

I packed my bags at once – had them taken to the railway station, where I registered them in the luggage office under a false name.

Then in the evening I returned to the town where I had rented a little house. The following day I sent for my baggage, which was delivered to my little house.

I said to myself, 'If I am not the victim of another new denunciation perhaps the police will leave me in peace.'

Thus I contrived to obtain 1½ months of peace but at what a price!

I almost never went out. I saw no-one. My meals were sent in from outside and I had engaged as servant a small creature who was totally deaf and almost entirely dumb. Her name was Cléopatra.

Plon-Plon was furious that his dear Cora should so be hounded. He wrote:

To think you should be victimised by the Government of Monte Carlo because France has expelled you!

and four days later:

Honestly, the Government of Monaco is giving itself airs as if it were a real Government and has the right to persecute you. It is odious!

Cora recalled in her memoirs, 'If every country I go to behaves like this to me I had better stay in the train, I thought.' But worse was to befall Cora before her life took a turn for the better. As she had expected, Plon-Plon's money was running out. He wrote her a touching farewell letter:

I have decided against you and against myself. You have always been charming and delighted me . . . I send you a last present.

But he could not bear to write the final Goodbye – a few days later he wrote:

I shall . . . shake your hand and embrace you with great joy if you wish my dear Cora.

Cora returned to Monte Carlo where Madame Laforêt joined her, and tried to dissuade her from gambling, for Cora was always unlucky at the tables. She fretted for her lost home, for her lost horses. She had no opportunity to use her immense talent for organising and entertaining. So the years fretted away, Cora always hoping to return to Paris.

Meanwhile, Duval, the would-be-witty and would-be- boulevar-dier, recovered from his self-inflicted wound and went on a Byronic 'pilgrimage'. On his return his mother did the best thing she had ever done for him. She died. Duval inherited a great fortune, pulled himself together and took over the business, of which he made a success and an enormous amount of money – acting like his father instead of having hysterics like his mother. He married a pretty little wife, with a substantial *dot*, and became the successful businessman nature intended him to be.

Cora's beautiful well-exercised body kept its youthful vigour, but her face betrayed the ravages of misfortune. One night an English gentleman named Julian Arnold left the Casino at Monte Carlo and crossed the Gardens on his way home to his villa. It was raining hard. He was surprised to find a woman sitting on the kerbstone, weeping pitifully. He stopped and asked what was the matter. In a mixture of English and French, she related her tale of woe. She had been turned out of her lodging, her luggage had been seized. She had no money, no home, no food. Mr Arnold asked her name and was thunderstruck when she answered: 'I am Cora Pearl.'

He called a cab and took her to his villa which he shared with two friends. All three treated Cora with the greatest courtesy and respect, one declaring gallantly 'Higher heads than mine have bowed to Cora Pearl.' Warmth, a good dinner and an eager audience revived Cora wonderfully. She entertained her hosts all the evening with gay stories of the dizzy goings-on in the Second Empire.

It was late when Mr Arnold bade Cora goodnight, lending her his dressing-gown and arranging for his housekeeper to escort her to the best bedroom. Finally, Mr Arnold retired alone to his library for a late reading session.

Presently Cora entered, looking happier and self-confident. She was wrapped in the dressing gown Arnold had lent her. As he rose from his chair, Cora, with a graceful gesture, let the dressing-gown slip to her feet. She was stark naked. 'A woman's vanity,' Cora murmured, 'should be my sufficient excuse – I could not sleep until I had shown you that, if Cora Pearl has lost everything else, she still retains a form of beauty which made her famous!'

It was Cora's only means of saying 'Thank you'.

Next day Cora, her confidence restored, resolved to try her luck once again at the Casino, despite Madame Laforêt's earnest

THE TRUTH ABOUT CORA PEARL

pleadings not to. In the days of her glory – in these same rooms, she had once won 30,000 francs and, continuing to play, finally lost 70,000 francs. Now, however, she was sure she was going to be lucky. She had only one five-franc piece to venture. She hesitated at the roulette table a long time before committing herself to placing her precious chip. There was a hubbub at the door. The manager, bowing obsequiously, was escorting a very important guest – a superbly-tailored figure with a *légion d'honneur* in his lapel and a pretty young wife clinging adoringly to his arm. They stopped at the roulette table. The important guest carelessly threw a handful of Napoléons and gold hundred-franc pieces on to the nearest number. Cora, holding her breath, carefully placed her five-franc chip. Across the green table their eyes met. It was Alexandre Duval.

The croupier called. The wheel spun. The wheel ceased to spin. Duval had won a fortune. Cora had lost her five francs.

16
Afterwards

And Cora finally did get back to her beloved Paris, which, like herself, was not what it had been. She finally settled in a comfortable third-floor apartment at 8 rue de Bassano where she remained for the rest of her life.

Madame Laforêt was totally arthritic by now. She and Cora were a pair of old troupers gallantly keeping up appearances. They played Cora's favourite card game of Chinese Bézique every day and lived quietly.

Faithful Salé, Cora could see, was dreaming of his native Provence. She proposed that he should return there to end his days in the sun. She still had odds and ends to sell. She proposed to raise a little capital for him. Would he not like to open a small restaurant in the Midi, or maybe a lively café?

But Salé would not take any money. He had his savings and, to tell the truth, he had always made a little bit as well on those huge food bills. And he grinned his audacious southern grin, for he knew Cora knew. It was true he longed to warm his wooden leg in the sun. And so, with a flourish of his crutches, Salé took his leave for good. With him went Cora's great days of Second Empire entertaining.

But Cora was still Cora, not made for a quiet life. She no longer gambled at the tables, but she could not resist engaging frequently in expensive litigation, always unsuccessfully.

Was it prudent Madame Laforêt who put Cora on to the study of *Volapük*, 'a new international language'? Cora planned to develop it commercially for the grand 1889 Paris Exhibition, renamed it

Corapük, amazed her teacher by her quick study, then, bored, dropped it altogether.

In a big hat, Cora went again to the races where her carriage was quickly surrounded by ageing beaux from the Jockey Club enjoying her jokes, and newcomers wondering what they were laughing about.

The truth is that there is an era to which one belongs and when it is over one belongs no more. In France the change was violently abrupt. Parisians were suddenly quite different. So were their clothes and their manners. So were their *cocottes*.

Cora, who still took great pride in her profession, and still received certain lovers, took a poor view of the new batch of Professionals. In her eyes, they did not begin to understand the basic principle of the art, which is *luxury*.

Before Cora died, the last of the great courtesans had appeared at the Folies Bérgères. She was an extraordinary Spanish Gypsy dancer name La Belle Otéro, with an hourglass figure, ramrod back, and passionate life-style which brought her a shower of wealthy lovers, loads of jewels and a Pacific Island from the Emperor of Japan. Otéro, who did everything to excess (even living to the age of ninety-seven, still upright as a lamp-post) used to boast of losing thirty million francs in one session at Monte Carlo.

Cora would have been interested in Otéro's fantastic all-diamond bolero, fringed and tied with large diamond tassels – so valuable that it had to be kept in the vaults of her Paris bank, and when she wore it on stage she was shadowed by armed guards. There were far worse scandals in her life, including real suicides, than in Cora's, but Otéro sailed through them, actually profiting from the publicity.

After 1880 Cora's financial situation deteriorated. She had already successfully sold her silver collection in 1877. She was not accustomed, nor was it in her nature, to economise. News of her plight reached her old friends, both of the Profession and the Jockey Club. Gifts of money arrived from the Professionals and once every month a charming middle-aged gentleman (always different) came to call on her with a cheque and a bouquet. Cora had always been generous with money and in entertaining. It was a pleasure to help her out now. Over a glass of wine and a biscuit they would chat of old times and sift the gossip. Despite the poisonous reports in some newspapers after her death, Cora was never in want in her last years.

At last, however, she was obliged to sell Beauséjour, radiant in her memory with all the fun and good fellowship of her best years. Her small château was so heavily mortgaged that it brought in very little money. So when Jules Levy, the publisher, asked her to write her memoirs she agreed because she always needed money.

Her superb health, which she had enjoyed all her life and which had contributed so lavishly to her success, broke down. She fell ill. The doctors diagnosed cancer of the intestine – then fatal. A devoted young doctor named Talaman cared for her with kindness and understanding. And she wrote her memoirs during this period, racking her brains to remember and be funny. She did not often remember precisely and she was seldom funny. She realized that everything had changed in France so much that she was describing a way of life remote as the moon. What is valuable in Cora's memoirs is her occasional comment – shrewd, wise and proud.

The personages in her life were recalled as she wrote. *Professor Crouch*, her father, whom she believed dead, was, in fact, alive and survived Cora by ten years. He had obtained fine jobs in America, including that of Conductor of the New York Opera House. But, as always, gave up and stumbled into poverty. He had joined and been wounded in the American Civil War, predictably on the romantic Confederate side, and finished up in the varnishing department of a Baltimore furnishing factory – cared for by social workers. He had married three more times in America and fathered twenty-nine children, none of whom, as far as we know, he attempted to maintain.

Mr Saunders, the diamond merchant from Bordeaux, who had inadvertently set Cora on the road to fame, doubtless continued to seduce little girls and trade in diamonds.

Robert Richard Bignell (Bluckel in her memoirs), improved his successful business, adding the equally profitable Trocadéro. He had really started Cora on her amazing career by taking her to see the Parade of Courtesans in the Bois de Boulogne. He had spotted a star which all too soon darted out of his orbit. He died two years after Cora, leaving over £20,000 – then a large fortune. Not bad for a country lad who began his working life as a cobbler's apprentice.

Victor Masséna, Duc de Rivoli, afterwards the Fifth Prince of Essling (Lasséma in the memoirs), was Cora's first link in her famous 'chain of gold'. He meant no harm in introducing her to gambling, for he loved her devotedly and never got over her. He dutifully married the Duchesse Paule-Furtado-Hein of Elchingham, to please his parents, but not before he was forty-six, for Cora haunted him. As she wrote, he was 'a kind good man'. He died in Paris in 1910.

Prince Achille Murat (Adrian Marut in the memoirs) predictably continued his crazy life of gambling, whoring and piling up debts on his wife's estates in Russia until, finally, he committed suicide in 1895 aged forty-eight – a bad egg.

Charles Auguste Louis Joseph, Duc de Morny, (Moray in the memoirs), was Cora's favourite lover and 'friend for ever'. The Second Empire, which he had so cleverly master-minded, had been the perfect setting for all his dazzling talents (diplomacy, intrigue, finance, theatre and womanising). He was not the illegitimate grandson of the great Talleyrand for nothing. Had he lived he would certainly have prevented Louis-Napoléon from stumbling into the fatal Franco–Prussian War.

Louis-Napoléon and Eugénie: Despite the insinuations of the gossip-mongers, Cora was never the Emperor's mistress, as her memoirs make clear. They were not in any way each other's cup of tea. Nor had Cora a high opinion of Eugénie.

After the débâcle, Queen Victoria gave the ex-Imperial family sanctuary in England, in Camden Place, Chislehurst, Kent. After two futile years, still persuading himself he might be recalled to the throne, Louis-Napoléon died there. Her martial appetite unappeased, Eugénie encouraged her son, the *'ex-bébé Empereur'*, now twenty-three, to volunteer in the South African War, where he was killed by a Zulu Assegai. Her consolation, she said, was that 'His wounds were all at the front.'

Eugénie now lived only for revenge. She survived until 1920 to exult, at the age of ninety-seven, in the defeat of Germany in the First World War.

'Plon-Plon', *Prince Napoléon* (Jean-Jean in the memoirs): At the death of the ex-Prince Imperial, he became at last the direct heir to the French throne. But there was no throne. The French did not want him. Nobody wanted him except his faithful neglected wife, Princess Clothilde, in whose arms he died five years after the death of his adored Cora.

Païva (the Countess Donnersmarck): After the fall of the Commune she returned to Paris and again occupied her undamaged Hollywood Palace in the Champs Elysées. The Donnersmarcks constantly dined at the German Embassy and continued to spy and intrigue for Bismarck. They were hated by the French. When, wearing jewels worth two million francs, she went to a performance of Offenbach's *Périchole* escorted by her husband, the audience booed her so loudly that they were obliged to leave the theatre.

The German Ambassador thereupon forced Thiers to invite them to dinner at the Elysée. But in 1878 MacMahon, who had succeeded Thiers, gave in to the will of the French people and had them banished.

The Countess of Donnersmarck could not bear to give up her Champs-Elysées Palace, and demanded to have it taken down (onyx staircase, painted ceilings and all) and returned to her in Silesia. For once she failed. There it still stands. The French loathe it, even as an architectural curiosity. The British took it over, using it as a library, then as a travellers' club.

Païva died in her husband's castle in Silesia in 1884. Donnersmarck married again, a German girl of good family by whom he had several children. There were dark stories of Païva's body, preserved in alcohol, being kept as a shrine in a locked attic in the castle.

History has its ironies. The Portuguese nobleman, Visconde Georges Albino Franco de Païva y Aranjo, whom Thérèse married for his title and deserted after their wedding night, is preserved in the name 'Hôtel Païva', her fantastic palace on the Champs-Elysées, by which it has always been known.

Hortense Schneider (Hermance Schalder in the memoirs) prudently saved when her salary as a star was high and kept the costly gifts of her admirers, so that she retired in comfort when she left the stage. She married an Italian adventurer (Conte Emile de Bianne), divorcing him at once when she found he was only after her money. Then she spent the rest of her life devotedly caring for her mentally unstable son by the consumptive Duc de Caderousse, her great love. She died in 1920 leaving everything she possessed to a theatrical orphanage.

Gustave Doré, devastated by the ruin of Paris and haunted by the fate of his six pug dogs (eaten during the Siege), spent most of his time in London where he was made much of, and where he was able to sell his pictures, in his own gallery. The death of his tenacious mother in 1881, which should have released him, only devastated him for good. He lost his old gaiety and walked on his hands no more. At last, longing for marriage, a home and children, he became engaged to a suitable young French lady. But just before his wedding day he had a stroke and died. He was just fifty-one. Who can guess what he and Cora, who had so much in common, might have made of marriage together?

Louise Michel: In Noumea conditions for political prisoners were horrific, and those trying to escape by swimming were eaten by sharks. Gambetta succeeded in forcing an amnesty in 1880, when Louise Michel, who seemed indestructible, returned to Paris, only to be arrested and jailed three more times for 'revolutionary anarchist activities.' Finally she sailed for England, where she earned her living teaching French. As a young student, Augustus John, then something of an anarchist himself, knew her and never forgot the wild exultation of this small white-haired old lady when in 1905 the first Russian Revolution broke out.

Charles Worth's clientèle changed after the Second Empire. He collected ornamental 'tears' for a hobby whilst his two sons carried on his business. Cora told him sadly, 'Paris has no patience with tears. All she cares about is smiles.' His magic was personal and died with him.

Alexandre Duval made a large fortune, branching out into an 'up-market' restaurant near the Chambre de Deputés and opening a cheap one in Fleet Street opposite the London Law Courts. He became an important social figure, a racing man, with a reputation for wit (for great wealth can do much). He fancied himself for his gallantry but proved he was no gentleman by referring to Cora as 'that disgusting harridan whom I would not touch with a pair of tongs.' He died in 1922.

Cora's old friend, Mother Superior Beneventura, now came often to sit with her. She begged Cora to let herself be cared for in the Convent Hospital, but Cora would not give up her independence. She selected Doré's golden goblet from her remaining few treasures to give her old friend in remembrance. The Mother Superior thought it was a chalice symbolising the nurturing breast of the Madonna, offering suck to the Holy Child. Cora explained that it was her own incomparable breasts modelled by an artist she had nearly married, as a gift for a lover to whom she had been devoted.

'It is a symbol of love, Madame Cora,' replied the Mother Superior, with her quick understanding smile, 'And there are many kinds of love. I shall treasure it.'

She helped Cora sort out what she had left, ready for the auctioneers, for Cora was determined to leave Madame Laforêt as much as she could. Everything was in exquisite order, though most of the items made no sense to anyone except herself.

'Enough,' Cora judged with an expert eye, 'to make a two-day sale at Drouot . . . Plenty of good house linen. I restocked after the Siege. My underwear – the best plain silk – blue, black and the colour of Shantung: *Voyez*, Madame Beneventura, it is only women who are not sure of themselves who wear fancy underwear . . .'

'I am always learning something new,' nodded the Mother Superior. 'Now, what about your pictures?'

'This is my favourite,' said Cora, 'the equestrian portrait by Émile de Lanzac – a better painter than chocolate-cream Winterhalter. It should fetch a good price.' (It was to be knocked down at a hundred francs.) 'And here is a dear little watercolour by my friend Blanche d'Antigny, "The Nile at Sunset." She bought my mansion in the rue de Chaillot when I needed money desperately. Then she went bankrupt herself, fled to Egypt, got smallpox there and died quite young. Poor Blanche!' (The watercolour fetched a derisory one franc and seventy-five centimes.)

'Now, this pearl necklace is false, Mother Beneventura, but this one is real and worth 20,000 francs,' (which is precisely what it fetched), 'My beautiful books – a collection of classics with Doré's marvellous wood engravings – and my bronzes . . . and my good ebony furniture . . . Here's my other bed – a Professional's showpiece. Look at the satin upholstery and the elaborate fringes. That will concentrate the attention of the virtuous housewives . . . What a lark!'

'And here,' went on Cora, her voice softening, 'is a memento from the past – the bow and arrows I carried as Cupidon in *Orphée aux Enfers*. Doré designed them. What would not my admirers have bid for them in the old days!' (They found no buyer in the auction and were included in a minor job lot.)

An English bishop called on Cora to implore her to make her peace with God before she died. Cora told him politely that she did not fear the other side; she had always lived by her principles and was confident of forgiveness.

Cora's memoirs were published in French in March 1886, four months before she died. Her publishers hoped to make a killing, for every lady in the Profession in Europe and America (not to mention the respectable matrons who thrived on scandal) were eager to lay their hands on a copy. When they did, they were all disappointed.

Near the end, Mother Superior Beneventura took Cora's now wasted hands in her own firm ones and said earnestly: '*Mon enfant*, the penalty for independence is loneliness. To have been as independent as you have been requires immense courage and an iron harnessing of emotion. This has been the source of your amazing energy and endurance. A family can be, should be, a comfort and a mainspring. Also, alas, it can be a brake and a positive handicap. If you had been one of my novices, what great project would I not have harnessed you to. For you have love to give, Madame Cora, which you have not yet given – and you can laugh at yourself. What a gift that is!'

Two days later, Mother Beneventura hurried in, beaming through her glasses. She was carrying a new magazine, *Les femmes du Jour*. 'Look at this Madame Cora! The first number – by Zi-Zim, whoever he may be – it's all about you and for once it is courteous and truthful! See, it absolves you from all blame for the Duval business – and applauds the fine work you did and the sacrifices you made for your hospital during the Siege.' In her strong Lorraine accent Mother Beneventura read out slowly:

We honour her and shall forgive her much because she did so much to help our wounded during the Siege, and with what devotion she herself nursed our unhappy militiamen. We honour her remembering the good in her and forgetting the bad . . .

'*Ma mère*,' whispered Eugénie Laforêt at the door of the apartment, making her farewell arthritic curtsey to the Mother Superior, 'I am glad for her sake. Only I know how hurt and desperate she was when the police and the press hounded her from country to country. We French are like that. First we adore and flatter what takes our fancy then we dash it to the ground and trample on it. I, who have been with her a lifetime, know her to be an exceptional woman – a star! Not only has she unbelievable strength of character, but also great kindness, and she is totally devoid of snobbery. As you must know, *ma mère*, luxury is the hallmark of our profession, but what she truly enjoyed most, was simply making people laugh.'

'A rare gift,' agreed the Mother Superior.

'The two men in her life who did her the most harm, *ma mère*, were both young, rich and spoiled – Prince Achille right at the beginning and Duval right at the end. The older ones loved and appreciated her and tried to protect her – the Duc de Rivoli and the Duc de Morny and Plon-Plon – they were like fathers to her . . . and I do believe that was what Madame Cora was looking for, for all her independence – a fond father she could entertain with her pranks.' Madame Laforêt dabbed her eyes. 'She is dying, *ma mère*, and I cannot think how I shall live without her.'

'You, *mon enfant*, shall be the one to close her eyes,' Mother Beneventura said quietly, gathering up her robes to go.

Cora's last entry in her jumbled memoirs reads:

It's finished – my memoirs! Many others will take up where I leave off – there will always be attractive girls as there will always be princes and diplomats – unemployed and capitalists – those with a heart and those who are crooks.

If gold Louis are made to roll and diamonds to glitter, I should not be reproached for having given these noble things their rightful destination. I glittered with one and rolled with the others.

I have never deceived anyone because I have never belonged to anyone.

My independence has been all my fortune. I have known no other happiness.

At the end she rallied and laughed: 'I am still Cora, but minus the Pearls.'

Let this be her Epitaph.

Index